popina® **book of baking**

popina®
book of baking

Isidora Popović

photography by Peter Cassidy

RYLAND
PETERS
& SMALL

LONDON NEW YORK

For my parents, Pavle and Rozalia

Design, Photographic Art Direction, and Prop Styling Steve Painter
Senior Editor Céline Hughes
Production Controller Toby Marshall
Art Director Leslie Harrington
Publishing Director Alison Starling

Food Stylist Linda Tubby
Indexer Hilary Bird

Popina logo and branding Igor Jocić

First published in the US in 2010
by Ryland Peters & Small, Inc.
519 Broadway, 5th Floor,
New York, NY 10012
www.rylandpeters.com

10 9 8 7 6 5 4 3 2 1

ISBN: 978 1 84597 965 2

Notes

- All spoon measurements are level, unless otherwise specified.
- All eggs are medium, unless otherwise specified. It is generally recommended that free-range eggs be used. Uncooked or partially cooked eggs should not be served to the very young, the very old, those with compromised immune systems, or to pregnant women.
- Ovens should be preheated to the specified temperature. Recipes in this book were tested using a convection oven. If using a regular oven, you may need slightly longer baking times.
- Sterilize preserving jars before use. Wash them in hot, soapy water and rinse in boiling water. Place in a large saucepan and then cover with hot water. With the lid on, bring the water to a boil and continue boiling for 15 minutes. Turn off the heat, then leave the jars in the hot water until just before they are to be filled. Invert the jars onto clean paper towels to dry. Sterilize the lids for 5 minutes, by boiling, or according to the manufacturer's instructions. Jars should be filled and sealed while they are still hot.

Library of Congress Cataloging-in-Publication Data

Popovic, Isidora.
  Popina book of baking / Isidora Popovic ; photography by Peter Cassidy.
    p. cm.
  Includes index.
  ISBN 978-1-84597-965-2
  1. Baking. 2. Popina (Bakery) 3. Natural foods. I. Title.
  TX763.P635 2010
  641.8'15--dc22
                              2009043904

contents

foreword

The first time I met Isidora Popović, her bakery business, Popina, had been up and running for no more than a few months. It was a week or two before Christmas and as I strolled down the Portobello Road in London's Notting Hill district, I noticed a new stall. Lured by its grace and charm—not something you'd necessarily expect to find in a market in those days—it was filled with different cakes and cookies wrapped up in cellophane, tied with ribbon, and laid out in baskets. Not only did they look gorgeous but yes, they also tasted tantalizing. The quality and generosity of ingredients shone through. A depth of spices or an unusual and arresting blend, a bitingly crisp texture achieved from the simple union of flour and water, or a tender juiciness from the judicious addition of fruits—here was a baker indeed, and with originality, flair, and attention to detail. Isidora hovering like a mother hen fussing over her chicks was far too busy to chat and I think I may have disgraced myself that day by trying far too many samples. I just couldn't resist, and coming back for more… and more… but Isidora was far too gracious to comment. Honor was, I hope, restored by the packages I bought for friends and family and of course myself for the coming holidays.

The next time was when I set out to find her at her bakery in London's East End. Isidora had entered a competition for Small Producers and I was the judge. Now if I tell you that over the years I have visited thousands of small producers in their units, you must believe that I am not exaggerating. And so you should also believe me when I tell you meeting Isidora in her "unit" was like no other. I had no idea that her unit was actually her apartment or to be accurate her apartment/kitchen/production unit/store room/packing room/office. I have no problem with that (you'd be amazed at some of the places I've visited) but seeing several ovens cramped into a living room and almost every inch used for the storage of pans, trays, or some-such baking equipment with Isidora seemingly oblivious to the situation and rising above it all, took my breath away. There she was exuding warmth, passion, total dedication, and an obvious hunger for success. Fiercely proud and hugely ambitious, she represented, as she told me without a moment's hesitation "food artistry from the soul."

In one way, not much has changed since then. With Isidora at the helm, the quality remains consistent whatever the scale or production or success. I may not bump into Isidora serving at farmers' markets any more but when I bite into one of her products, I think of her and smile. I am delighted that she has succeeded in her stated ambition to deliver to every customer "the whole experience of taste, texture, and the visual" and now there's the added bonus of sharing with home cooks her recipes in this book.

Henrietta Green

introduction

I was born in Serbia, in a town called Novi Sad on the river Danube. In those days there were no big supermarkets in Serbia, so every day my mother went to the market where local farmers, cheesemongers, butchers, and fisherman brought their produce grown, made, or caught either in surrounding farms or in mountains deeper in the country. She always prepared breakfast, lunch, and dinner from scratch using the fresh ingredients she had bought that day. To this day, when I work on a recipe, I keep the picture of this childhood market in my head as a guiding image: the most amazing palette of colors bathed in sunshine, seasonal fruit and vegetables with their inviting smells, the hustle and bustle of market life—a real cornucopia.

I used to love watching my mother cook—she was so inventive with flavors and recipes. In the fall we picked fruit from which we made jams and compotes; we cooked tomatoes to make and store their sauce; we pickled cabbage, cucumbers, and bell peppers in the colors of the rainbow; we collected and dried nuts; we bought meat to make sausages and cure ham; and we dried flowers and herbs for the winter. Food and cooking weren't merely a necessity, they were a passion and an identity to be passed with pride to the next generations.

I started Popina in 1999 after completing an art degree at Goldsmiths in London. I had just designed an art project based on food and I felt so passionately about food that I wanted to share this and develop my interest. A great opportunity arose when, after a long wait, I got a pitch on Portobello Market in Notting Hill. With financial help and huge support from Prince Charles' The Prince's Trust, I set up Popina as a business and started trading. The company name was chosen because the word means "eatery" in Latin and suggests a welcoming place to eat. In true London style, Popina's recipes have always reflected a mixture of cultural influences and culinary inspiration.

In the early days I was baking cookies at home and bringing them to the busy market to sell. My greatest driving force and encouragement came from my customers, who loved our treats and came religiously to buy them. In its ten years, Popina's recipes have won many prestigious food awards and been enjoyed by food-lovers in the UK and abroad.

Popina is about imagination, seasonality, and a love of making great food, simply. My inspiration comes from a respect for nature and the constant need to create, learn, and be challenged. This book is a selection of my favorite recipes, some of which were among the first on that market stall ten years ago; others you can still buy today.

I sincerely hope you enjoy making the recipes as much as I did devising them, and I urge you to use this book as a canvas for your own creations.

Isidora Popović

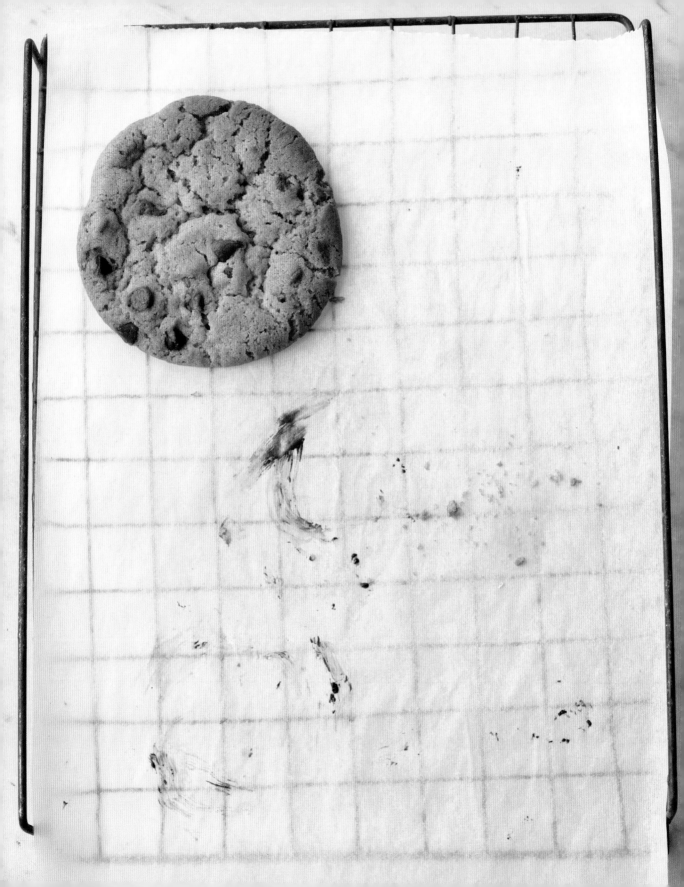

popina
cookies,
biscotti,
& bars

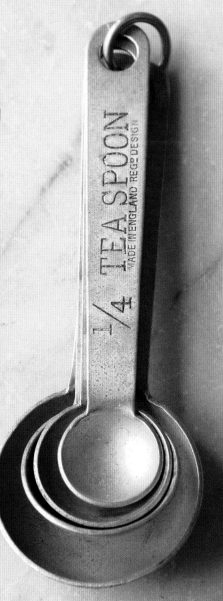

oat, ginger, and golden raisin cookies

Fruity, with warm tones of ginger—best enjoyed warm from the oven.

7 tablespoons unsalted butter, at room temperature

¾ cup packed light brown sugar

1 tablespoon corn syrup

1 egg

1½ cups all-purpose flour

½ teaspoon baking powder

⅓ cup jumbo (flaked) oats

½ cup crystallized ginger, chopped

½ cup golden raisins

1–2 baking sheets, greased

Makes about 12

Cream the butter and sugar in a mixing bowl until light and fluffy. Add the syrup and egg and mix well. Mix the flour, baking powder, and oats together in a separate bowl, then mix into the wet ingredients. Finally, mix in the ginger and raisins.

Roll the dough into a log 2 inches in diameter, wrap in plastic wrap, and refrigerate for about 1 hour.

Preheat the oven to 325°F.

Remove the dough from the refrigerator and unwrap it. Cut into disks about ¾ inch thick. Arrange the disks on the prepared baking sheet(s), spacing them well apart as they will spread when they are baking.

Bake in the preheated oven for about 20–25 minutes until the cookies are pale gold. Remove from the oven and let cool for a few minutes, then serve warm. Store in an airtight container for up to 1 week.

pecan and cranberry cookies

Lovely sweet pecans contrasting with the sharpness of dried cranberries. This is my favorite winter cookie.

7 tablespoons unsalted butter, at room temperature

¾ cup packed light brown sugar

1 tablespoon corn syrup

a few drops of pure vanilla extract

1 egg

1½ cups all-purpose flour

½ teaspoon baking powder

¼ cup chopped pecans

¼ cup dried cranberries

1–2 baking sheets, greased

Makes about 12

Cream the butter and sugar in a mixing bowl until light and fluffy. Add the syrup, vanilla, and egg and mix well. Mix the flour and baking powder together in a separate bowl, then mix into the wet ingredients. Finally, mix in the pecans and cranberries.

Roll the dough into a log 2 inches in diameter, wrap in plastic wrap, and refrigerate for about 1 hour.

Preheat the oven to 325°F.

Remove the dough from the refrigerator and unwrap it. Cut into disks about ¾ inch thick. Arrange the disks on the prepared baking sheet(s), spacing them well apart as they will spread when they are baking.

Bake in the preheated oven for about 20–25 minutes until the cookies are pale gold. Remove from the oven and let cool for a few minutes, then serve warm. Store in an airtight container for up to 1 week.

chocolate chip cookies

You can use chocolate chips for these cookies or simply chop up some good chocolate bars. Eat the cookies warm while the chocolate is still molten.

1 stick unsalted butter, at room temperature

¾ cup plus 1 tablespoon packed light brown sugar

1 tablespoon corn syrup

a few drops of pure vanilla extract

1 egg

1½ cups plus 1 tablespoon all-purpose flour

½ teaspoon baking powder

½ cup chopped bittersweet chocolate (or use chips)

½ cup chopped milk chocolate (or use chips)

1–2 baking sheets, greased

Makes about 12

Cream the butter and sugar in a mixing bowl until light and fluffy. Add the syrup, vanilla, and egg and mix well. Mix the flour and baking powder together in a separate bowl, then mix into the wet ingredients. Finally, mix in the chopped chocolate.

Roll the dough into a log 2 inches in diameter, wrap in plastic wrap, and refrigerate for about 1 hour.

Preheat the oven to 325°F.

Remove the dough from the refrigerator and unwrap it. Cut into disks about ¾ inch thick. Arrange the disks on the prepared baking sheet(s), spacing them well apart as they will spread when they are baking.

Bake in the preheated oven for about 20–25 minutes until the cookies are pale gold. Remove from the oven and let cool for a few minutes, then serve warm. Store in an airtight container for up to 1 week.

oat and raisin cookies

A classic cookie made the Popina way—chewy and packed full of oats. Make a few extra dough disks, freeze, and save for baking on a lazy weekend afternoon (but let thaw for 15 minutes first).

10 tablespoons unsalted butter, at room temperature

⅔ cup plus 1 tablespoon packed light brown sugar

1 egg

1 cup all-purpose flour

½ teaspoon baking powder

½ teaspoon ground cinnamon

1½ cups rolled oats

¾ cup raisins

1–2 baking sheets, greased

Makes about 12

Cream the butter and sugar in a mixing bowl until light and fluffy. Add the egg and mix well. Mix the flour, baking powder, cinnamon, and oats together in a separate bowl, then mix into the wet ingredients. Finally, mix in the raisins.

Roll the dough into a log 2 inches in diameter, wrap in plastic wrap, and refrigerate for about 1 hour.

Preheat the oven to 325°F.

Remove the dough from the refrigerator and unwrap it. Cut into disks about ¾ inch thick. Arrange the disks on the prepared baking sheet(s), spacing them well apart as they will spread when they are baking.

Bake in the preheated oven for about 20–25 minutes until the cookies are pale gold. Remove from the oven and let cool for a few minutes, then serve warm. Store in an airtight container for up to 1 week.

cornmeal, cherry, and nut biscotti

This is an excellent gluten- and dairy-free recipe that I created years ago for my customers on Portobello Road. The biscotti are crumbly, irresistible, and perfect with a strong coffee.

1 cup cornmeal

½ cup rice flour

1½ teaspoons baking powder

½ cup sugar

2 eggs, separated

3 tablespoons apple juice

¼ cup dried sour cherries (or dried cranberries)

¼ cup golden raisins

¼ cup pistachio kernels

¼ cup shelled hazelnuts

a baking sheet, lined with parchment paper

Makes about 20

Preheat the oven to 300°F.

Mix the cornmeal, rice flour, baking powder, and sugar.

In a mixing bowl, beat the egg yolks until pale, then add the apple juice and cornmeal mixture and stir to combine.

In a separate bowl, whisk the egg whites until they form stiff peaks, then gently fold into the cornmeal mix. Finally, stir in the cherries, raisins, pistachios, and hazelnuts.

Spoon the mixture onto the center of the prepared baking sheet and shape it into a reasonably flat log about 3 inches wide (you can use the parchment paper to help you roll the dough).

Bake in the preheated oven for about 30 minutes. To check if it's ready, press very lightly on top of the log and if it springs back you can take it out of the oven. If it still feels very firm, leave it in for a few more minutes.

Using a large, serrated bread knife, slice the log into ⅜-inch slices. The best way to cut this type of gluten-free pastry is just to press the knife down quickly so that the biscotti doesn't crumble too much.

Lay the slices on the baking sheet and return to the hot oven for 10 minutes, turning them halfway through cooking. When they are pale gold, remove from the oven and let cool for a few minutes. Store in an airtight container for up to 2 weeks.

fig, apricot, and nut biscotti

These double-baked crisp cookies are packed with dried fruit and nuts, and are made lighter without butter. They are best enjoyed with a strong coffee or dipped in some vanilla ice cream for a sweet treat.

1½ cups all-purpose flour

1½ teaspoons baking powder

½ cup sugar

¼ cup pistachio kernels

¼ cup shelled hazelnuts

¼ cup golden raisins

4 dried apricots, quartered

4 dried figs, quartered

freshly grated zest of 1 small unwaxed lemon

2 eggs, lightly beaten

a baking sheet, lined with parchment paper

Makes about 28

Preheat the oven to 300°F.

Sift the flour and baking powder into a mixing bowl. Stir in the sugar, pistachios, hazelnuts, raisins, apricots, figs, and lemon zest.

Pour in the eggs and mix well until you get a dough-like mixture. Bring the dough together into a ball in your hands and transfer it to the prepared baking sheet.

Flour your hands and roll the dough into a log (you can use the parchment paper to help you roll the dough). Flatten it slightly so that it is about 3 inches wide.

Bake in the preheated oven for about 30 minutes. To check if it's ready, press very lightly on top of the log and if it springs back you can take it out of the oven. If it feels firm, leave it in the oven for a few more minutes. When it is ready, remove from the oven and let cool for about 10 minutes.

Using a large, serrated bread knife, slice the log into ¼-inch slices. Lay the slices on the baking sheet and return to the hot oven for 10 minutes, turning them halfway through cooking. When they are pale gold, remove from the oven and let cool for a few minutes. Store in an airtight container for up to 2 weeks.

white chocolate and fig cookies

These are super indulgent cookies—soft, chewy, and fruity, with creamy white chocolate chips. Heavenly. Try to buy soft, dried figs as they are the easiest to bake with. If, however, you can only find tougher dried figs, you will have to cut off their hard stalks before you add them to the cookie dough.

3 tablespoons unsalted butter, at room temperature

⅓ cup plus 1 tablespoon sugar

a few drops of pure vanilla extract

1 egg

½ cup soft, dried figs, chopped

⅓ cup chopped white chocolate (or use chips)

1 cup all-purpose flour

1½ teaspoons baking powder

1–2 baking sheets, lined with parchment paper

Makes about 15

Preheat the oven to 325°F.

Cream the butter and sugar in a mixing bowl until light and fluffy. Add the vanilla and egg and mix well. Stir in the figs and chopped chocolate. Mix the flour and baking powder together in a separate bowl, then gently fold into the wet ingredients.

Take a generous teaspoon of the cookie dough and place on one of the prepared baking sheets. Flatten slightly, then repeat with the remaining dough, spacing the dough balls well apart as they will spread when they are baking.

Bake in the preheated oven for about 25 minutes, or until the cookies are pale gold. Remove from the oven and let cool for a few minutes. Store in an airtight container for up to 1 week.

ginger and chili caramel cookies

These addictive cookies are drizzled with hot caramel, so you can explore your artistic side when it comes to decorating them! With a generous dose of crystallized ginger and bit of chili heat, they are not for the faint-hearted.

3 tablespoons unsalted butter, at room temperature

½ cup sugar

1 egg

½ cup crystallized ginger, finely chopped

1 cup all-purpose flour

1½ teaspoons baking powder

2 teaspoons ground ginger

Chili caramel

½ cup sugar

a pinch of ground cayenne or hot chili powder (or more if you like the heat!)

1–2 baking sheets, greased

Makes about 15

Preheat the oven to 325°F.

Cream the butter and sugar in a mixing bowl until light and fluffy. Add the egg and mix well, then stir in the crystallized ginger. Mix the flour, baking powder, and ground ginger in a separate bowl, then gently fold into the wet ingredients.

Take a generous teaspoon of the dough and place on one of the prepared baking sheets. Flatten it slightly, then repeat this process with the remaining dough, spacing the dough balls well apart as they will spread when they are baking.

Bake in the preheated oven for about 25 minutes, or until the cookies are golden. Remove from the oven and let cool while you make the chili caramel.

To make the chili caramel, put the sugar in a heavy-based saucepan over medium heat. The sugar can burn quite easily (which can render the caramel bitter), so stir it often and keep a close eye on it. After a few minutes, the sugar should have completely melted. Remove from the heat and stir in the cayenne or chili powder. Be very careful when handling caramel as it can easily burn you. Use it immediately before it starts to harden.

Using a spoon, drizzle the caramel over the cookies any way you like. The caramel sets extremely quickly. When it has set, remove the cookies from the baking sheet. Store in an airtight container for up to 1 week, but be warned that in humid conditions the caramel can seep into the cookies.

pineapple, coconut, and lemon cookies

I recommend making the candied pineapple in advance, as it keeps well for weeks and you can use it any time to make a batch of these cookies. You can also store the cooking syrup, which has a wonderful pineapple flavor and which I use to season my breakfast cereal.

6½ tablespoons unsalted butter, at room temperature

¾ cup plus 2 tablespoons sugar, or 6 oz. pineapple syrup (see method)

2 eggs

finely grated zest of 1 unwaxed lemon

1 cup desiccated coconut or finely grated fresh coconut

2 cups all-purpose flour

2 teaspoons baking powder

Candied pineapple

14 oz. canned pineapple pieces in juice, drained

2½ cups sugar

2 baking sheets, greased

Makes about 24

To make the candied pineapple, put the drained pineapple pieces and sugar in a saucepan over low/medium heat. The sugar, along with the natural juices from the pineapple, will form a syrup and the edges of the pineapple will become translucent. Stir occasionally, then take the pan off the heat after 30 minutes—the pineapple pieces will still have a bite to them and will be full of flavor.

Let cool for 15 minutes. Pick out the pineapple pieces and chop them up if they are still too big. Use them straight-away or put them in a lidded jar or airtight container along with just a few tablespoons of the syrup. You can also store the syrup in separate jar or container to use another day.

Preheat the oven to 325°F.

Cream the butter and sugar (or 6 oz. of the reserved pineapple syrup) in a mixing bowl until light and fluffy. Add the eggs and mix well, then stir in the lemon zest, candied pineapple, and coconut. Mix the flour and baking powder in a separate bowl, then gently fold into the wet ingredients.

Take a generous teaspoon of the dough and place on one of the prepared baking sheets. Flatten it slightly, then repeat this process with the remaining dough, spacing the dough balls well apart as they will spread when they are baking.

Bake in the preheated oven for about 25 minutes, or until golden. Remove from the oven and let cool for a few minutes. Store in an airtight container for up to 1 week.

spelt, chocolate, and hazelnut cookies

I love spelt flour and it works incredibly well with this combination of hazelnuts and chocolate.

5 tablespoons unsalted butter, at room temperature

½ cup sugar

1 egg

a few drops of pure vanilla extract

1 cup plus 2 tablespoons spelt flour

1 teaspoon baking powder

⅓ cup shelled hazelnuts, roughly chopped

⅓ cup chopped bittersweet chocolate (or use chips)

⅓ cup chopped milk chocolate (or use chips)

1–2 baking sheets, greased

Makes about 17

Preheat the oven to 325°F.

Cream the butter and sugar in a mixing bowl until light and fluffy. Add the egg and vanilla and mix well. Mix the flour and baking powder in a separate bowl, then gently fold into the wet ingredients. Finally, mix in the hazelnuts and chopped chocolate.

Take a generous teaspoon of the cookie dough and place on one of the prepared baking sheets. Flatten it slightly, then repeat this process with the remaining dough, spacing the dough balls well apart as they will spread when they are baking.

Bake in the preheated oven for about 25 minutes, or until the cookies are deep golden. Remove from the oven and let cool for a few minutes. Store in an airtight container for up to 1 week.

walnut shortbreads

Crumbly and buttery with a strong taste of walnuts. If you have time, you can very lightly roast the walnuts to give these delightful cookies that extra punch.

¾ cup shelled walnuts

6 tablespoons unsalted butter, at room temperature

¼ cup sugar

a few drops of pure vanilla extract

1 cup all-purpose flour

confectioners' sugar or vanilla sugar, to dust

1–2 baking sheets, greased

Makes about 16

Preheat the oven to 250°F.

If you have time, put the walnuts on a baking sheet and roast in the preheated oven for 10 minutes, then roughly chop one half and finely chop the other (or blitz in a food processor). If you are short of time, skip this roasting step and just chop the nuts as above.

Cream the butter, sugar, and vanilla in a mixing bowl until light and fluffy. Stir in the walnuts, then gently fold in the flour until well mixed.

Roll the dough into a log 1¼ inches in diameter, then cut into disks about ¾ inch thick. Roughly roll each disk into a ball—it should be about the size of a walnut. Arrange the dough balls on the baking sheet(s), spacing them well apart as they will spread when they are baking.

Bake in the preheated oven for about 30 minutes— they should still be slightly soft in the middle. Remove from the oven and dust with confectioners' or vanilla sugar. Store in an airtight container for up to 2 weeks.

hazelnut macaroons

This is another dairy- and gluten-free cookie. If you prefer, you can use ground almonds in place of the rice flour—it will make the macaroons a touch softer. They are crunchy on the outside, chewy in the middle, and very, very nutty.

1 cup plus 2 tablespoons blanched hazelnuts

2 egg whites

¾ cup sugar

⅓ cup rice flour (or ground almonds)

a few drops of pure vanilla extract

a baking sheet, greased

Makes about 20

Preheat the oven to 250°F.

Put the hazelnuts on a baking sheet and roast in the preheated oven for about 15 minutes, or until very pale gold. Grind them finely in a spice grinder or food processor, leaving a few chunkier pieces.

In a mixing bowl, mix the egg whites and sugar just to combine, then add the ground hazelnuts, rice flour, and vanilla. Cover the bowl with plastic wrap and refrigerate for 30 minutes.

Take the mixture out of the refrigerator and stir through with a spoon. Take a generous teaspoon of the dough and place on the prepared baking sheet. Flatten it slightly, then repeat this process with the remaining dough, spacing the dough balls slightly apart as they may spread when they are baking.

Bake in the preheated oven for about 25 minutes, or until the macaroons are very pale gold. They should still be slightly soft in the middle. Remove from the oven and let cool for a few minutes. Store in an airtight container for up to 1 week.

gingerbread men and women

These are great fun to make with children—they can get creative and dress up the gingerbread people with different types of chocolate, nuts, or dried fruit. For a less dressy person, stick to white chocolate.

1⅓ cups all-purpose flour

1 teaspoon baking powder

1½ teaspoons ground ginger

5 tablespoons unsalted butter, chilled and cubed

3 tablespoons sugar

3 tablespoons honey

1 teaspoon water

about 2 oz. white chocolate, melted (or any other chocolate, nuts, and dried fruit), to decorate

gingerbread men cutters in sizes of your choice

a baking sheet, greased

Makes about 4 grown-ups

Preheat the oven to 325°F.

Put the flour, baking powder, ginger, butter, sugar, and honey in a food processor and pulse until you get crumbs. Add the water and mix until a ball of dough has formed.

Transfer the dough to a lightly floured surface and roll out with a rolling pin until about ¼ inch thick. Cut out people with your chosen cutters and place on the baking sheet.

Bake in the preheated oven for 20–30 minutes, then let cool before decorating.

To decorate, pipe molten white chocolate clothes onto the gingerbread people, or accessorize with chopped nuts and dried fruit. Store in an airtight container for up to 2 weeks.

easter egg cookies

These are great-looking chocolate cookies studded with dried fruit and nuts. You can decorate them by scattering the nuts and dried fruit over them haphazardly or spend time over an artistic design. Either way, they make thoughtful Easter gifts.

1 cup plus 2 tablespoons all-purpose flour

1 teaspoon baking powder

1½ tablespoons unsweetened cocoa powder

¼ cup packed light brown sugar

4 tablespoons unsalted butter, chilled and cubed

2½ tablespoons honey

1 teaspoon water

To decorate

3½ oz. white chocolate, chopped

¼ cup chopped almonds

¼ cup pistachio kernels

¼ cup chopped pecans (optional)

¼ cup dried cranberries, chopped

a 4-inch high, egg-shaped cookie cutter

a baking sheet, greased

Makes 5

Preheat the oven to 325°F.

Put the flour, baking powder, cocoa, sugar, butter, and honey in a food processor and pulse until you get crumbs. Add the water and mix until a ball of dough has formed.

Transfer the dough to a lightly floured surface and roll out with a rolling pin until about ¼ inch thick. Cut out egg shapes with the cookie cutter and place on the baking sheet.

Bake in the preheated oven for 25 minutes, then let cool before decorating.

To decorate, put the chocolate in a heatproof bowl over a saucepan of barely simmering water. Do not let the base of the bowl touch the water. Stir until melted.

Brush the melted chocolate over one side of each cookie with a pastry brush, then scatter the nuts and cranberries over the top. If you prefer, you can arrange the decoration in a pattern.

Let the chocolate cool and set before serving. Store in an airtight container away from sunlight for up to 2 weeks.

granola bars

These tempting, wholesome granola bars take almost no time to make and are perfect get-ahead treats for those weekday mornings when you don't have time to make breakfast.

¾ cup plus 2 tablespoons packed light brown sugar

⅛ cup corn syrup

9 tablespoons unsalted butter

⅓ cup apple juice

1 cup jumbo (flaked) oats

1 cup rolled oats

¾ cup golden raisins

⅛ cup pumpkin seeds

⅛ cup sunflower seeds

an 8 x 12-inch baking pan (2½ inches deep), lined with parchment paper

Makes 12 large bars

Preheat the oven to 350°F.

Put the sugar, syrup, butter, and apple juice in a saucepan and gently bring to a boil. Remove from the heat and stir in the remaining ingredients until well mixed. Transfer to the prepared baking pan and spread evenly.

Bake in the preheated oven for 15–20 minutes, then remove from the oven and let cool.

Lift the parchment paper, granola and all, up and out of the pan, and transfer to a cutting board. Cut into bars and store in an airtight container for up to 1 week.

florentines

These nutty, fruity nibbles dipped in bittersweet chocolate are perfect after-dinner Christmas treats served with coffee or tea. We sell them gift-wrapped for stocking stuffers. If you have a mini-muffin pan, you can bake the florentines in this so that you get perfect circles, but it's just as easy to make them by hand and bake them on a sheet.

4 tablespoons unsalted butter

⅛ cup sugar

¼ cup honey

½ cup all-purpose flour

¼ cup mixed peel

¼ cup dried cranberries

½ cup golden raisins

⅛ cup flaked almonds, plus extra to sprinkle

⅛ cup chopped walnuts

⅛ cup chopped pecans

2½ oz. bittersweet chocolate, chopped

1–2 baking sheets, greased

Makes about 20

Preheat the oven to 300°F.

Put the butter, sugar, and honey in a saucepan over medium heat and gently bring to a boil. Do not let the ingredients burn. When it reaches boiling point, stir until the sugar has dissolved completely, then remove from the heat.

Stir in the flour, mixed peel, cranberries, raisins, almonds, walnuts, and pecans. Mix until well combined. Let cool for a while before handling.

Take a generous teaspoon of the mixture, roughly roll into a ball, and place on one of the prepared baking sheets. Flatten it gently, then repeat this process with the remaining mixture, spacing the disks apart as they may spread when they are baking. Sprinkle a few flaked almonds over each florentine.

Bake in the preheated oven for 15 minutes. Remove from the oven and let cool.

In the meantime, put the chocolate in a heatproof bowl over a saucepan of barely simmering water. Do not let the base of the bowl touch the water. Stir until melted. Dip one side of each florentine in the bowl of melted chocolate and let set, chocolate side up, on a cooling rack. Store in an airtight container for up to 2 weeks.

popina
sweet
tarts

tart crusts

These three crusts are used, individually or together, in all of Popina's tart recipes. They are so simple that I would encourage you to experiment with different seasonal fruit fillings and make your own masterpiece! If you have any dough left over, freeze it for next time.

sweet dough

2 cups all-purpose flour

1 stick unsalted butter, chilled and cubed

5 tablespoons sugar

1 egg

Makes enough to line a 9-inch round pan

Put the flour, butter, and sugar in a food processor and blitz until you get crumbs. Add the egg and mix again. Take the dough out of the processor and bring together into a ball. If you prefer, you can make the dough by hand, but it's easier to do this if the butter is very finely chopped.

Put the dough on a lightly floured surface and roll with a rolling pin until ⅛ inch thick.

Turn to the tart recipe you are using and continue following the instructions.

chocolate dough

1¾ cups all-purpose flour

3 tablespoons unsweetened cocoa powder

1 stick unsalted butter, chilled and cubed

5 tablespoons sugar

1 egg

Makes enough to line a 9-inch round pan

Put the flour, cocoa, butter, and sugar in a food processor and blitz until you get crumbs. Add the egg and mix again. Take the dough out of the processor and bring together into a ball. If you prefer, you can make the dough by hand, but it's easier to do this if the butter is very finely chopped.

Put the dough on a lightly floured surface and roll with a rolling pin until ⅛ inch thick.

Turn to the tart recipe you are using and continue following the instructions.

biscuit dough

3 tablespoons unsalted butter, at room temperature

a scant ½ cup sugar

1 egg

1½ teaspoons baking powder

¾ cup all-purpose flour

Makes enough to line a 9-inch round pan

Put the butter and sugar in a mixing bowl and mix with an electric whisk to combine.

Mix in the egg and baking powder with the whisk, then gently fold in the flour by hand until evenly combined.

Turn to the tart recipe you are using and continue following the instructions.

apple and plum tart

An absolutely classic Popina recipe and always on our menu! When we first produced these tarts on our farmers' market stall, we sold hundreds every weekend. I recommend using strongly flavored, tart apples like Winesaps, and a sweet plum variety like Santa Rosa. There is plenty of fruit filling, which makes it wonderfully juicy. Best eaten either warm from the oven or chilled with some custard.

1 Sweet Dough recipe
(see page 40)

1 Biscuit Dough recipe
(see page 40)

2 Winesap apples,
cored and sliced

10 Santa Rosa plums, pitted
and halved

3 tablespoons apricot jam,
to glaze (optional)

*a 9-inch loose-bottomed
fluted tart pan, greased*

Makes about 8 slices

Preheat the oven to 325°F.

Line the tart pan with the Sweet Dough and trim the excess neatly around the edges. Spoon the Biscuit Dough into the tart crust and spread evenly. Scatter the apples and plums all over the top.

Bake in the preheated oven for 40 minutes. When the tart is ready, the fruit will have sunk a little and the biscuit dough will have risen up in parts and be golden. Remove from the oven and let cool for a few minutes.

In the meantime, put the apricot jam, if using, in a small saucepan and heat gently until melted and runny. Brush the jam all over the tart filling with a pastry brush and leave for a few more minutes before serving. Alternatively, serve it straight from the refrigerator with a helping of custard.

rhubarb custard and crumble tartlets

Creamy rhubarb custard tarts with buttery cookie crumbs on top. If you like, you can skip the crumble step and crush 6 oz. good, storebought shortbread cookies instead. For an extra helping of decadence, serve with custard. You can even make more of the mashed rhubarb, then push it through a strainer to make a lovely coulis for pouring onto the tartlet. Using red rhubarb will make it a fantastic vibrant pink.

1 Sweet Dough recipe
(see page 40)

Crumble

¾ cup all-purpose flour

3 tablespoons unsalted
butter, chilled and cubed

3 tablespoons sugar

Rhubarb custard

12 oz. rhubarb, trimmed and
sliced into small pieces

⅔ cup sugar

3 eggs

a few drops of pure
vanilla extract

½ cup heavy cream

a baking sheet, greased

*6 x 3½-inch loose-bottomed
fluted tartlet pans, greased*

Makes 6

Preheat the oven to 350°F.

To make the crumble, mix the flour, butter, and sugar in a food processor. Bring the dough together with your hands and transfer to a lightly floured surface. Roll with a rolling pin until about ⅛ inch thick, then place on the prepared baking sheet. Bake in the preheated oven for 15 minutes, or until pale gold. Remove from the oven (leaving the oven on) and let cool completely, then crush into crumbs and set aside.

Line the tartlet pans with the Sweet Dough and trim the excess neatly around the edges. Blind bake for 10 minutes, or until pale gold. Leave the oven on.

To make the rhubarb custard, put the rhubarb in a roasting pan, sprinkle over the sugar, and give it a stir. Cover with foil and roast in the hot oven for about 20–25 minutes, until soft. Remove from the oven, let cool for a few minutes, then blitz roughly in a food processor or mash with a fork.

Reduce the oven temperature to 300°F.

Whisk the eggs and vanilla together. Pour the cream into a saucepan over low heat and gently bring to a boil, stirring frequently. Remove from the heat and whisk in the eggs and vanilla and then the rhubarb until well combined.

Fill each tartlet crust up to the top with rhubarb custard and bake in the hot oven for 15–20 minutes, until the filling no longer wobbles when you shake the tartlet. Remove from the oven and scatter crumble over the top. Let cool slightly before serving or even better, serve chilled.

fig, grape, and frangipane tartlets

The best time to make these is late summer to early fall when figs are in season and at their most flavorful. If you can also get hold of black Muscat grapes, you'll have a rhapsody of flavors!

1 Sweet Dough recipe (see page 40)

3 tablespoons unsalted butter, at room temperature

¼ cup sugar

1 large egg

⅓ cup ground almonds

3 tablespoons all-purpose flour

4 drops of almond extract

6 fresh figs, halved and stalks slightly trimmed

about 24 red (or black Muscat) grapes

6 x 4-inch loose-bottomed fluted tartlet pans, greased

Makes 6

Preheat the oven to 325°F.

Line the tartlet pans with the Sweet Dough and trim the excess neatly around the edges. Refrigerate while you make the filling.

Put the butter, sugar, egg, ground almonds, flour, and almond extract in a food processor and mix until you get a soft cream.

Fill each tartlet crust up to the top with almond cream and spread evenly, then arrange 2 fig halves and about 4 grapes on top. Bake in the preheated oven for about 20–25 minutes. When the tartlets are ready, the almond cream will be golden. Remove from the oven and let cool for a few minutes.

nectarine and summer berry tart

This is my favorite summer tart—it's bursting with all kinds of berries, plus nectarines, which make everything taste extra summery! I would encourage you, whenever possible, to buy your fruit directly from your local farmers' market where the growers bring just-picked fruits that are perfectly ripe and full of flavor.

1 Sweet Dough recipe
(see page 40)

1 Biscuit Dough recipe
(see page 40)

8 oz. nectarines, pitted
and sliced

a handful of blueberries

a handful of raspberries

a handful of strawberries,
hulled and halved

3 tablespoons apricot jam,
to glaze (optional)

*a 9-inch loose-bottomed
fluted tart pan, greased*

Makes about 8 slices

Preheat the oven to 325°F.

Line the tart pan with the Sweet Dough and trim the excess neatly around the edges. Spoon the Biscuit Dough into the tart crust and spread evenly. Scatter the nectarines, then the berries all over the top.

Bake in the preheated oven for 40 minutes. When the tart is ready, the fruit will have sunk a little and the biscuit dough will have risen up in parts and be golden. Remove from the oven and let cool for a few minutes.

Put the apricot jam, if using, in a small saucepan and heat gently until melted and runny. Brush the jam all over the tart filling with a pastry brush and leave for a few more minutes before serving with a dollop of crème fraîche.

rustic plum tart

This recipe was created with late summer in mind. It's very simple, light, and fruity, and really you can make it with any ripe fruit you have a glut of. A variation that works particularly well, though, is apple and cinnamon, which is the winter partner to the summer plum.

½ cup sugar

1 egg

2½ tablespoons peanut oil

¼ cup whole milk

1 cup plus 1 tablespoon all-purpose flour

1 teaspoon baking powder

a few drops of pure vanilla extract

6 large plums, pitted and halved

2 tablespoons apricot jam, to glaze (optional)

an 8-inch springform pan, baselined with parchment paper

Makes about 6 slices

Preheat the oven to 350°F.

Put the sugar and egg in a mixing bowl and mix with an electric whisk. Add the oil, milk, flour, baking powder, and vanilla and mix again until combined. Transfer to the prepared springform pan and spread evenly. Sit the plums, cut side up, over the mixture.

Bake in the preheated oven for about 30 minutes, or until deep golden. Remove from the oven and let cool for just a few minutes.

In the meantime, put the apricot jam, if using, in a small saucepan and heat gently until melted and runny. Brush the jam all over the tart with a pastry brush and leave for a few more minutes before serving.

Variation: Substitute ½ teaspoon ground cinnamon for the vanilla, and 1 Golden Delicious apple, cored and sliced, for the plums. Follow the recipe as above.

chocolate and pistachio tartlets

This recipe is made in two parts and there is something incredibly satisfying about covering the chocolate filling in the rich ganache. I recommend that you use good-quality chocolate, at least 70% cocoa solids if possible. The variation at the bottom of the page is for creamy white chocolate ganache tartlets with just a hint of coffee.

1 Chocolate Dough recipe, or plain Sweet Dough if you prefer (see page 40)

a handful of pistachio kernels, chopped, to decorate

Chocolate filling

⅓ cup sugar

1 egg

½ cup all-purpose flour

½ teaspoon baking powder

2 teaspoons unsweetened cocoa powder

1 tablespoon unsalted butter

1 oz. bittersweet chocolate, chopped

2 tablespoons water

Chocolate ganache

1½ oz. bittersweet chocolate, finely chopped

1½ oz. milk chocolate, finely chopped

⅔ cup heavy cream

6 x 3½-inch loose-bottomed fluted tartlet pans, greased

Makes 6

Preheat the oven to 350°F.

Line the tartlet pans with the Chocolate Dough and trim the excess neatly around the edges. Refrigerate while you make the filling.

To make the chocolate filling, put the sugar and egg in a mixing bowl and beat with an electric whisk until pale yellow. Gently fold in the flour, baking powder, and cocoa powder. In a heatproof bowl, melt the butter and chocolate over a pan of simmering water, then add to the mixing bowl. Add the water and mix well.

Spoon about 1½ tablespoons chocolate filling into each tartlet crust. Bake in the preheated oven for 15 minutes. Remove from the oven and let cool for 10 minutes.

To make the chocolate ganache, put the chocolate in a mixing bowl. Put the cream in a saucepan and gently bring to a boil over low heat, stirring frequently. Pour into the mixing bowl and whisk until you get a smooth cream.

Pour the chocolate ganache into the tartlets, then scatter the pistachios over the top. Refrigerate and serve chilled.

Variation: To make White Mocha Tartlets, the instructions are as above but you need to add 1 teaspoon instant coffee to the 2 tablespoons water (hot) in the Chocolate Filling. You will need to make a White Chocolate Ganache: dissolve ½ teaspoon instant coffee in 1 tablespoon hot water and put in a mixing bowl with 4 oz. finely chopped white chocolate. Heat ½ cup heavy cream and gently bring to a boil, then pour into the mixing bowl and whisk until smooth.

chocolate and chestnut tart

Creamy, rich chestnuts paired with a double helping of chocolate—
what more can you ask for in a decadent dessert!

1 Chocolate Dough recipe
(see page 40)

Chestnut filling

2 tablespoons unsalted
butter, at room temperature

2 tablespoons sugar

1 egg

½ cup all-purpose flour

1 teaspoon baking powder

1 oz. cooked chestnuts,
chopped

3 tablespoons heavy cream,
chilled

2 tablespoons cold water

3 oz. canned sweetened
chestnut purée

Chocolate ganache

1½ oz. milk chocolate,
finely chopped

1½ oz. bittersweet chocolate,
finely chopped

¾ cup heavy cream

*a 9-inch loose-bottomed
fluted tart pan, greased*

Makes about 8 slices

Preheat the oven to 350°F.

Line the tart pan with the Chocolate Dough and trim the excess neatly around the edges. Refrigerate while you make the filling.

To make the chestnut filling, cream the butter and sugar in a mixing bowl until light and fluffy. Add the egg and mix well. Mix the flour, baking powder, and chestnuts together in a separate bowl, then mix into the wet ingredients. Finally, slowly add the cream and water and incorporate well.

Remove the tart crust from the refrigerator and spread the chestnut purée over the base. Spoon the chestnut filling on top and spread evenly. Bake in the preheated oven for 20 minutes, or until the dough has risen and is pale gold. Remove from the oven and let cool for a few minutes. Trim the top of the filling if it has risen too much.

To make the chocolate ganache, put the chocolate in a mixing bowl. Put the cream in a saucepan and gently bring to a boil over low heat, stirring frequently. Pour into the mixing bowl and whisk until you get a smooth cream. Let cool for 10 minutes, then pour it into the tart. Refrigerate and serve chilled.

chocolate, pear, and hazelnut tart

This stunning dessert is fit for your most discerning dinner guests, but it is also simple enough to make for a sophisticated picnic.

1 Chocolate Dough recipe (see page 40)

1 Biscuit Dough recipe (see page 40)

1 large pear, peeled, halved, and cored

3 tablespoons hazelnuts (blanched if you like), roughly chopped

2 tablespoons apricot jam (optional)

Chocolate and hazelnut cream

3 oz. bittersweet chocolate, finely chopped

3 oz. milk chocolate, finely chopped

¾ cup light cream

6 tablespoons hazelnuts, roughly chopped and lightly toasted in a dry skillet

a 9-inch loose-bottomed fluted tart pan, greased

Makes 8–12 slices

Preheat the oven to 325°F.

Line the tart pan with the Chocolate Dough and trim the excess neatly around the edges. Refrigerate while you make the filling.

To make the chocolate and hazelnut cream, put the chocolate in a mixing bowl. Put the cream in a saucepan and gently bring to a boil over low heat, stirring frequently. Pour into the mixing bowl and whisk until you get a smooth cream, then stir in the hazelnuts. Gently fold the Biscuit Dough into the chocolate mixture and mix well. Remove the tart crust from the refrigerator and pour in the chocolate and hazelnut cream.

Cut the pear into about 12 slim wedges and arrange in a circle on top of the tart filling. Sprinkle the hazelnuts over the top. Bake in the preheated oven for about 25 minutes. To check if it's ready, insert a skewer into the center of the tart—if it comes out clean you can take it out of the oven. If not, leave it in the oven for a few more minutes.

Put the apricot jam, if using, in a small saucepan and heat gently until melted and runny. Brush the jam roughly over the tart (avoiding the hazelnuts) with a pastry brush and leave for a few more minutes before serving.

pecan and bourbon tartlets

Nutty, with the subtle flavor of bourbon coming through, these smart, irresistible little tarts are perfect for winter entertaining. Bake a batch at Christmastime to round off a festive feast.

1 Sweet Dough recipe
(see page 40)

18 pecan halves, to decorate

Date filling

2 oz. Medjool dates, pitted
(or any soft date)

2 tablespoons heavy cream

1 tablespoon water

2 tablespoons unsalted
butter, melted

2½ tablespoons light brown
sugar

1 egg

a few drops of vanilla extract

½ cup all-purpose flour

1 teaspoon baking powder

Pecan bourbon filling

1 tablespoon bourbon
whiskey

3 tablespoons light brown
sugar

¼ cup corn syrup

1 egg, beaten

1½ tablespoons unsalted
butter, melted

½ cup chopped pecans

*6 x 3½-inch loose-bottomed
fluted tartlet pans, greased*

Makes 6

Preheat the oven to 350°F.

Line the tartlet pans with the Sweet Dough and trim the excess neatly around the edges. Refrigerate while you make the filling.

To make date filling, blitz the dates to a paste in a food processor or simply chop them very finely. Mix with the cream and water and set aside.

Put the butter and sugar in a mixing bowl and mix well, then add the egg, vanilla, flour, and baking powder. Finally, add date mixture and fold in well.

Remove the tartlet shells from the refrigerator and spoon about 1½ tablespoons of the date filling into them. Bake in the preheated oven for 15 minutes, then remove from the oven (leaving the oven on).

In the meantime, make the pecan bourbon filling. Put the bourbon, sugar, and syrup in a mixing bowl and mix well. Add the egg, mix, then stir in the melted butter and pecans.

Spoon the pecan bourbon filling on top of the tartlets and spread evenly. Decorate with 3 pecan halves and return to the oven for another 10 minutes. Remove from the oven and let cool before serving.

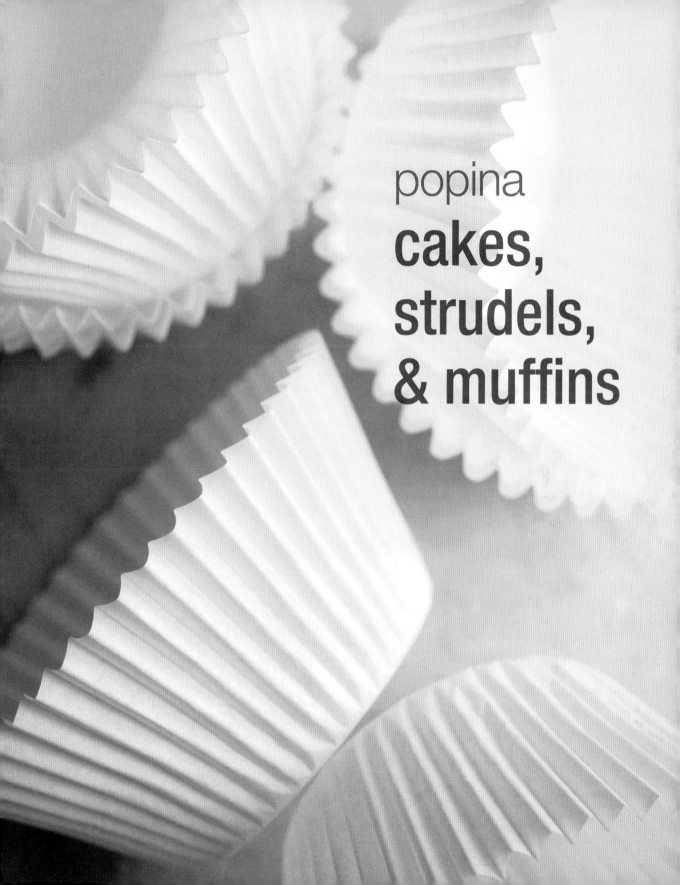

popina
cakes,
strudels,
& muffins

very chocolate cake

This is a seriously rich and creamy gluten-free cake created especially for chocoholics. Use good chocolate with at least 70% cocoa solids.

9 oz. bittersweet chocolate, chopped

7 tablespoons unsalted butter

2 eggs

⅔ cup sugar

⅛ cup rice flour

1½ teaspoons baking powder

¼ cup whole milk

Chocolate frosting

9 tablespoons unsalted butter, at room temperature

1¼ cups confectioners' sugar

10 oz. cream cheese

1 tablespoon unsweetened cocoa powder

an 8-inch springform pan, baselined with parchment paper

Makes 10–12 slices

Preheat the oven to 325°F.

Put the chocolate and butter in a heatproof bowl over a saucepan of barely simmering water. Do not let the base of the bowl touch the water. Stir until melted, then let cool slightly before using.

Put the eggs and sugar in a mixing bowl and whisk until they have formed a thick foam. Add the rice flour and baking powder and mix, then stir in the melted chocolate and butter. Finally, gently stir in the milk. Pour into the prepared springform pan and bake in the preheated oven for 40 minutes. To check if it's ready, insert a skewer into the center of the cake—if it comes out clean you can take it out of the oven. If not, leave it in the oven for a few more minutes. Let the cake cool completely before removing the pan.

In the meantime, make the chocolate frosting. Put the butter, sugar, cream cheese, and cocoa powder in a food processor and blitz until smooth. Alternatively, put the ingredients in a mixing bowl and whip by hand until smooth. Spread the frosting over the cake with a palette knife.

popina carrot cake

This exceptionally light and moist gluten- and dairy-free carrot cake was mastered with love by Popina's own Matt Gruninger.

5 eggs, separated

finely grated zest and freshly squeezed juice of 2 unwaxed lemons

2 tablespoons Kirsch (optional)

1¼ cups sugar

8 oz. carrots, grated

2 cups ground hazelnuts

2 teaspoons baking powder

½ cup cornstarch

Lemon icing

2 cups confectioners' sugar

freshly squeezed juice of 3 lemons (plus a little grated zest, to decorate)

a 10-inch springform pan, baselined with parchment paper

Makes about 12 slices

Preheat the oven to 350°F.

Put the egg yolks, lemon zest and juice, Kirsch (if using), sugar, carrots, hazelnuts, and baking powder in a mixing bowl and whisk to combine. Sift in the cornstarch and fold it in gently.

In a separate, grease-free bowl, whisk the egg whites until stiff peaks form. Fold the egg whites into the cake mix very gently, then transfer the batter to the prepared springform pan. Bake in the preheated oven for 45 minutes, or until springy in the touch. To check if it's ready, insert a skewer into the center of the cake—if it comes out clean you can take it out of the oven. If not, leave it in the oven for a few more minutes. Let the cake cool completely before removing the pan.

In the meantime, make the lemon icing. Mix the sugar and lemon juice well to achieve a runny icing. Pour the icing over the cake, letting it drip down the sides. Sprinkle with grated lemon zest.

The cake improves in flavor over a couple of days.

lemon loaf with white chocolate frosting

The rich, citrussy base and creamy white chocolate frosting are fabulously matched in this perfect teatime cake.

4 tablespoons unsalted butter, at room temperature

⅔ cup sugar

2 eggs

1 cup all-purpose flour

1½ teaspoons baking powder

finely grated zest and freshly squeezed juice of 2 unwaxed lemons

White chocolate frosting

5 oz. white chocolate, chopped, plus extra, grated, to decorate

⅛ cup heavy cream

a nonstick 6 x 4½ x 3-inch loaf pan, lined with parchment paper

Makes about 6 slices

Preheat the oven to 325°F.

Put the butter and sugar in a mixing bowl and mix well with an electric whisk. Add the eggs and whisk for a couple of minutes until pale and fluffy. Gently fold in the flour and baking powder. Finally, stir in the lemon zest and juice until well mixed.

Pour the mixture into the prepared loaf pan and bake in the preheated oven for 25 minutes. When it's ready, the cake will be a rich golden color and springy to the touch. Remove it from the oven and let cool before frosting.

In the meantime, make the white chocolate frosting. Put the chocolate in a mixing bowl. Put the cream in a saucepan and gently bring to a boil over low heat, stirring frequently. Pour into the mixing bowl and whisk until you get a smooth cream. Let cool for a couple of minutes, then refrigerate for 15 minutes to stiffen.

Spread the frosting on top of the cake and sprinkle some grated chocolate over it.

cranberry, sherry, and vine fruit cake

We serve this cake as an alternative to the traditional English Christmas cake. It is loaded with sherry-soaked fruits, walnuts, and cranberries.

4 tablespoons unsalted butter, at room temperature

¼ cup packed light brown sugar

1 tablespoon molasses

2 small eggs, beaten

½ cup all-purpose flour

1½ teaspoons baking powder

½ teaspoon ground cinnamon

freshly grated zest of 1 unwaxed orange

⅓ cup fresh or frozen cranberries

2 tablespoons chopped walnuts

Sherry-soaked fruits

⅔ cup dark raisins

¾ cup golden raisins

½ cup mixed peel

3 tablespoons sherry (dry, if possible)

3 tablespoons apple juice

Topping

½ cup apricot jam

⅔ cup fresh or frozen cranberries

½ cup walnut halves

an 8-inch nonstick springform pan

Makes 10–12 slices

Prepare the sherry-soaked fruits at least 24 hours in advance. Put the raisins, mixed peel, sherry, and apple juice in a bowl. Mix, cover, and let rest for at least 24 hours.

When you are ready to make the cake, preheat the oven to 350°F.

Put the butter, sugar, and molasses in a mixing bowl and mix well. Fold in the eggs, then add the flour, baking powder, cinnamon, orange zest, cranberries, and walnuts. Finally, fold in about 7 oz. of the soaked fruit, setting the rest aside for the topping. Pour the mixture into the prepared pan and bake in the preheated oven for 30 minutes, or until deep golden and springy to the touch. Remove from the oven and let cool in the pan.

To make the topping, put the apricot jam in a saucepan and gently bring to a boil over low heat, stirring frequently. Add the cranberries and cook for a few minutes, until their skins just begin to crack. Remove from the heat and stir in the walnuts and the remaining sherry-soaked fruit. Mix well and spoon on top of the cake. Cover the cake evenly and press very slightly to fix it in place. Let rest for a few hours before serving.

stollen

This is a labor-intensive but rewarding traditional Christmas sweet filled with rum-soaked fruits and plenty of marzipan.

finely grated zest of
1 unwaxed lemon

8 oz. marzipan

1 egg, beaten

7 tablespoons unsalted
butter, melted

1 cup confectioners' sugar

Rum-soaked fruits

1½ cups golden raisins

1½ cups mixed peel

⅓ cup dark or golden rum

Stollen dough

1 tablespoon quick-acting
dry yeast

⅓ cup sugar

½ cup plus 1 tablespoon
whole milk, warmed

1 large egg yolk

1½ sticks unsalted butter,
at room temperature

3¾ cups bread flour

*a baking sheet, lined with
parchment paper*

Makes 2 stollen

Prepare the rum-soaked fruits at least 24 hours in advance. Put the raisins, mixed peel, and rum in a bowl. Mix, cover, and let rest for at least 24 hours.

When you are ready to make the stollen dough, stir the yeast and sugar into the warm milk and set aside for 5 minutes.

Put the egg yolk, butter, and flour in a mixing bowl and add the yeast mixture. Mix until you get a smooth dough, then transfer to a lightly floured surface and knead for 5 minutes. The dough should be soft but not sticky. If it is sticky, add a little flour and knead again. Return the dough to the mixing bowl, dust in flour, cover, and let rise for 1 hour in a warm place. The dough should increase significantly in size.

Stir the lemon zest into the rum-soaked fruits, then uncover your mixing bowl and pour in the soaked fruits. Knead the dough again to incorporate and evenly distribute the fruits. Divide the dough in two, cover, and let rise for another 40 minutes in a warm place.

Take one ball of dough and roll it out with a rolling pin into a rough square about ¼ inch thick. Take half the marzipan and roll it into a tube slightly shorter than the square of dough. Place it along one side of the dough and start to roll the dough up from that side. Keep the sides tucked in as you roll. Repeat with the other ball of dough and remaining marzipan. Brush the beaten egg over the stollen. Cover and let rise for another 30 minutes in a warm place.

Preheat the oven to 400°F.

Put the logs on the prepared baking sheet and bake in the preheated oven for 10 minutes, then reduce the heat to 375°F and bake for another 20 minutes. Remove from the oven and brush the stollen generously with melted butter. Dust with confectioners' sugar and let cool.

chocolate and hazelnut strudel

This is my version of the traditional strudel made with a rich, buttery yeast dough. I recommend toasting the hazelnuts lightly, which will give it a stronger nutty flavor.

Strudel dough

1½ teaspoons quick-acting dry yeast

⅓ cup whole milk, warmed

3 tablespoons warm water

4 tablespoons unsalted butter, at room temperature

1 egg yolk

⅓ cup sugar

a few drops of pure vanilla extract

2 teaspoons unsweetened cocoa powder

2 cups bread flour

Hazelnut filling

1 cup hazelnuts, lightly toasted in a dry skillet

⅓ cup whole almonds

1 cup confectioners' sugar, plus extra to dust

3 tablespoons water

2 drops of pure vanilla extract

a baking sheet, lined with parchment paper

Makes about 10 slices

To make the strudel dough, put the yeast in a large glass measuring cup, then slowly whisk in the warm milk and water and set aside for 5 minutes. Don't worry if it looks like it's curdling.

Cream the butter, egg yolk, sugar, vanilla, and cocoa powder in a mixing bowl until light and fluffy. Add the flour and yeast mixture and mix in by hand until you get a smooth dough. Transfer to a well floured surface and knead for a couple of minutes. The dough should be soft but not sticky. If it is sticky, add a little flour and knead again. Return the dough to the mixing bowl, cover, and let rise for 1½ hours in a warm place. The dough should increase in size.

In the meantime, make the hazelnut filling. Put all the ingredients in a food processor and blitz until you have a loose paste.

Uncover your mixing bowl and transfer the ball of dough to the well floured surface. (You may find it helpful to roll the dough directly on a sheet of parchment paper, which will make rolling up the strudel easier.) Knead for a couple of minutes, then roll out with a rolling pin to a rectangle about 14 x 12 inches.

Spread the hazelnut filling over the dough with a palette knife, leaving a 1-inch border around the sides and back edge. Start rolling the strudel from the front. The dough will be soft but it should be quite elastic. Do not press or roll the dough too tightly, as it will need some give to expand while baking. Press the ends to seal and fold them underneath the strudel. Transfer to the prepared baking sheet, seam side down. Let rise for another hour.

Preheat the oven to 400°F.

Bake in the preheated oven for 10 minutes, then reduce the heat to 350°F and bake for another 15–20 minutes. The strudel should be springy to the touch. Let cool, then dust with confectioners' sugar.

poppyseed strudel

If you go anywhere in Eastern Europe, you will come across this cake in one form or another. It is delicious eaten with a glass of cold milk.

Strudel dough

1½ teaspoons quick-acting dry yeast

¼ cup whole milk, warmed

3 tablespoons warm water

1⅔ cups bread flour

5 tablespoons unsalted butter, at room temperature

1 egg yolk

¼ cup sugar

Poppyseed filling

¾ cup poppyseeds

¾ cup confectioners' sugar

3 tablespoons water

a baking sheet, lined with parchment paper

Makes about 8–10 slices

To make the strudel dough, put the yeast in a large glass measuring jug, then slowly whisk in the warm milk and water and set aside for 5 minutes. Don't worry if it looks like it's curdling.

Put the flour, butter, egg yolk, and sugar in a mixing bowl and mix well. Add the yeast mixture and mix with your hands until you get a smooth dough. Transfer to a well floured surface and knead for a couple of minutes. The dough should be soft but not sticky. If it is sticky, add a little flour and knead again. Return the dough to the mixing bowl, cover, and let rise for 1 hour in a warm place. The dough should increase significantly in size.

Turn the risen dough out onto the floured surface and knead again for 5 minutes, then let rest while you make the filling.

To make the poppyseed filling, put all the ingredients in a coffee or spice grinder and blitz until you have a loose paste.

Transfer the rested dough to the floured surface again. (You may find it helpful to roll the dough directly on a sheet of parchment paper, which will make rolling up the strudel easier.) Roll it out with a rolling pin to a square about 10 x 10 inches.

Spread the poppyseed filling over the dough with a palette knife, leaving a 1-inch border around the sides and back edge. Start rolling the strudel from the front. The dough will be soft but it should be quite elastic. Do not press or roll the dough too tightly, as it will need some give to expand while baking. Press the ends to seal and fold them underneath the strudel. Transfer to the prepared baking sheet, seam side down. Let rise for a further 45 minutes.

Preheat the oven to 350°F.

Bake the strudel in the preheated oven for 25–30 minutes. The strudel should be springy to the touch and be a deep golden color.

pumpkin and cinnamon phyllo strudel

Here's the perfect recipe for early fall—a crumbly, heavenly phyllo strudel made with creamy, sweet pumpkin and a hint of cinnamon. I make this with large sheets of phyllo pastry, which I find in Middle Eastern shops or the freezer aisle of my local supermarket. I just let it defrost for 1 hour before I start. If you can't find such large sheets, simply overlap your sheets to make the correct size and remember that you'll need more to begin with.

a small pie pumpkin, about ½ lb.

½ teaspoon ground cinnamon

¼ cup sugar

1½ tablespoons vegetable oil

3 large sheets of thick phyllo pastry (18 x 13 inches)

confectioners' sugar, to dust

a baking sheet, greased

Makes 6 slices

Preheat the oven to 325°F.

Peel and seed the pumpkin, then grate the flesh and squeeze out any excess water. Put in a bowl and mix with the cinnamon and sugar.

Take one sheet of phyllo pastry, lay it on the prepared baking sheet, and lightly brush with oil. Place a second sheet on top and lightly brush with oil. Repeat with the third sheet.

Spoon the pumpkin filling along one longer side of the phyllo sheets, leaving a 1-inch gap on either side and spreading the filling about 2 inches wide. Fold the longer side of the pastry, nearest the filling, about 1 inch in, then roll the phyllo pastry up, tucking in the sides as you go. When the strudel is baking, the filling will soften and some juice might seep out, so tucking in the sides ensures that not too much juice is lost.

Brush the top of the strudel with a little more oil and bake in the preheated oven for 25 minutes. The strudel should be pale gold. Remove from the oven and let cool for 5 minutes. Dust liberally with confectioners' sugar and serve warm.

summer fruit and white chocolate muffins

These are very moist muffins packed full of fruit and nuggets of white chocolate. An indulgent treat with a mid-morning coffee.

2 eggs

5 tablespoons sugar

3 tablespoons vegetable oil (or peanut or sunflower)

a few drops of pure vanilla extract

1 cup plus 3 tablespoons all-purpose flour

1½ teaspoons baking powder

1 large nectarine, pitted and sliced

½ cup strawberries, hulled and quartered

2½ oz. white chocolate, chopped

Topping

½ nectarine, pitted and sliced

½ cup raspberries

3 strawberries, hulled and quartered

light brown sugar, to sprinkle

a muffin pan, lined with 6 muffin cases

Makes 6

Preheat the oven to 350°F.

Put the eggs, sugar, oil, and vanilla in a mixing bowl and mix well until you have a smooth liquid. Mix the flour and baking powder together in a separate bowl, then mix into the wet ingredients. Stir in the nectarines, strawberries, and white chocolate until evenly mixed.

Fill each muffin case about two-thirds full with batter. Scatter the fruit for the topping over the muffins and finish with a sprinkling of sugar. Bake in the preheated oven for about 25 minutes. Do not be tempted to open the oven door halfway through baking as it might cause the muffins to sink. When they are ready, they should be well risen and springy to the touch.

Muffins are always best eaten warm from the oven, but if you have some left over you can refresh them with a quick flash in the microwave. Store in an airtight container for 2–3 days.

spelt, carrot, apple, and pumpkin seed muffins

I love these spelt muffins—light, nutty, and wholesome with hints of cinnamon and apple.

2 eggs

5 tablespoons sugar

3 tablespoons vegetable oil (or peanut or sunflower)

1 cup plus 2 tablespoons spelt flour

1½ teaspoons baking powder

1 teaspoon ground cinnamon

1 small carrot, grated

1 small apple, peeled, cored, and diced

2 tablespoons pumpkin seeds

Topping

3 tablespoons pumpkin seeds

light brown sugar, to sprinkle

a muffin pan, lined with 6 muffin cases

Makes 6

Preheat the oven to 350°F.

Put the eggs, sugar, and oil in a mixing bowl and mix well until you have a smooth liquid. Mix the flour, baking powder, and cinnamon together in a separate bowl, then mix into the wet ingredients. Stir in the carrot, apple, and pumpkin seeds until evenly mixed.

Fill each muffin case about two-thirds full with batter. Scatter the pumpkin seeds for the topping over the muffins and finish with a sprinkling of sugar. Bake in the preheated oven for about 25 minutes. Do not be tempted to open the oven door halfway through baking as it might cause the muffins to sink. When they are ready, they should be well risen and springy to the touch.

Muffins are always best eaten warm from the oven, but if you have some left over you can refresh them with a quick flash in the microwave. Store in airtight container for 2–3 days.

cranberry, orange, and pistachio muffins

These muffins look so appealing when you pull them out of the oven on a cold winter's morning. The tart tang of the cranberries ensures that the muffins are not too sweet.

2 eggs

5 tablespoons sugar

3 tablespoons vegetable oil (or peanut or sunflower)

finely grated zest and freshly squeezed juice of 1 unwaxed orange

1 cup plus 2 tablespoons all-purpose flour

2½ teaspoons baking powder

¾ cup fresh or frozen cranberries

Topping

⅓ cup fresh or frozen cranberries

a handful of pistachio kernels, chopped

light brown sugar, to sprinkle

a muffin pan, lined with 6 muffin cases

Makes 6

Preheat the oven to 350°F.

Put the eggs, sugar, oil, orange zest, and juice in a mixing bowl and mix well until you have a smooth liquid. Mix the flour and baking powder together in a separate bowl, then mix into the wet ingredients. Stir in the cranberries until evenly mixed.

Fill each muffin case about two-thirds full with batter. Scatter the cranberries and pistachios for the topping over the muffins and finish with a sprinkling of sugar. Bake in the preheated oven for about 25 minutes. Do not be tempted to open the oven door halfway through baking as it might cause the muffins to sink. When they are ready, they should be well risen and springy to the touch.

Muffins are always best eaten warm from the oven, but if you have some left over you can refresh them with a quick flash in the microwave. Store in airtight container for 2–3 days.

chocolate truffle brownies

This is our award-winning brownie—soft and creamy, made with the best chocolate, and with a similar texture to truffles. Irresistible.

8 oz. bittersweet chocolate (at least 70% cocoa solids)

6½ tablespoons unsalted butter

3 eggs

⅔ cup sugar

½ cup all-purpose flour

cocoa powder, to dust

an 8-inch square baking pan, lined with parchment paper

Makes about 9 squares

Preheat the oven to 300°F.

Put the chocolate and butter in a heatproof bowl over a saucepan of barely simmering water. Do not let the base of the bowl touch the water. Stir until melted. Set aside to cool.

Put the eggs and sugar in a mixing bowl and whisk until pale and creamy. Sift in the flour and fold in gently. Finally, fold in the molten chocolate and mix until smooth.

Pour the batter into the prepared baking pan and bake in the preheated oven for 15 minutes. The brownies should have risen slightly.

Let cool completely, then dust with cocoa powder. Cut into 9 squares and serve.

cherry chocolate truffle brownies

Go the extra mile on these decadent brownies and soak the dried cherries in rum or whiskey overnight before starting.

8 oz. bittersweet chocolate (at least 70% cocoa solids)

6½ tablespoons unsalted butter

3 eggs

⅔ cup sugar

½ cup all-purpose flour

¼ cup dried sour cherries

cocoa powder, to dust

an 8-inch square baking pan, lined with parchment paper

Makes about 9 squares

Preheat the oven to 300°F.

Put the chocolate and butter in a heatproof bowl over a saucepan of barely simmering water. Do not let the base of the bowl touch the water. Stir until melted. Set aside to cool.

Put the eggs and sugar in a mixing bowl and whisk until pale and creamy. Sift in the flour and fold in gently. Fold in the molten chocolate and mix until smooth. Stir in the cherries. Pour into the prepared pan and bake in the preheated oven for 15 minutes, or until slightly risen.

Let cool. Dust with cocoa, cut into 9 squares and serve.

double orange truffle brownies

A classic combination for those who love mixing orange with chocolate, with mixed peel and natural orange oil.

8 oz. bittersweet chocolate (at least 70% cocoa solids)

6½ tablespoons unsalted butter

3 eggs

⅔ cup sugar

½ cup all-purpose flour

2 tablespoons mixed peel

3 drops of natural orange oil

cocoa powder, to dust

an 8-inch square baking pan, lined with parchment paper

Makes about 9 squares

Preheat the oven to 300°F.

Put the chocolate and butter in a heatproof bowl over a saucepan of barely simmering water. Do not let the base of the bowl touch the water. Stir until melted. Set aside to cool.

Put the eggs and sugar in a mixing bowl and whisk until pale and creamy. Sift in the flour and fold in gently. Fold in the molten chocolate and mix until smooth. Stir in the mixed peel and orange oil. Pour into the prepared pan and bake in the preheated oven for 15 minutes, or until slightly risen.

Let cool. Dust with cocoa, cut into 9 squares and serve.

white chocolate and coffee truffle brownies

There's a little love story behind this recipe: my good friends told me on their wedding day that they used to buy each other bags of these brownies when they were courting and subsequently fell in love. I like to think that the brownies had something to do with it...

8 oz. bittersweet chocolate (at least 70% cocoa solids)

6½ tablespoons unsalted butter

2 teaspoons instant coffee

3 tablespoons boiling water

3 eggs

⅔ cup sugar

½ cup all-purpose flour

2½ oz. white chocolate, chopped (or use chips)

cocoa powder, to dust

an 8-inch square baking pan, lined with parchment paper

Makes about 9 squares

Preheat the oven to 300°F.

Put the chocolate and butter in a heatproof bowl over a saucepan of barely simmering water. Do not let the base of the bowl touch the water. Stir until melted. Set aside to cool.

Put the instant coffee and boiling water in a cup and stir until dissolved. Set aside.

Put the eggs and sugar in a mixing bowl and whisk until pale and creamy. Stir in the coffee. Sift in the flour and fold in gently, then fold in the molten chocolate and mix until smooth. Finally, stir in the chopped white chocolate.

Pour the batter into the prepared baking pan and bake in the preheated oven for about 15 minutes. The brownies should have risen slightly.

Let cool completely, then dust with cocoa powder. Cut into 9 squares and serve.

popina
savory straws & nibbles

gouda and hazelnut nibbles

Cheesy and nutty nibbles, great for aperitifs and parties.

1 cup plus 1 tablespoon all-purpose flour

5 tablespoons unsalted butter, chilled and cubed

½ cup grated Gouda (or cheddar) cheese

1 teaspoon salt

½ teaspoon baking soda

3 tablespoons roughly ground hazelnuts

2–3 tablespoons water

1–2 baking sheets, greased

Makes about 30–40

Preheat the oven to 300°F.

Put the flour, butter, cheese, salt, baking soda, and hazelnuts in a food processor and pulse until the mixture resembles crumbs. Add the water and pulse until the mixture comes together into a dough.

Transfer the dough to a lightly floured surface. Roll into a log about 1¼ inches in diameter, wrap in plastic wrap, and refrigerate for about 1 hour.

Remove the dough from the refrigerator and unwrap it. Cut into disks about ½ inch thick. Arrange the disks on the baking sheet(s), spacing them slightly apart as they may spread when they are baking.

Bake in the preheated oven for about 20 minutes, or until pale gold. Remove from the oven and let cool. Store in an airtight container for up to 2 weeks.

blue cheese and celery nibbles

Blue cheese and celery are a perfect pair. For the best result, use a strong cheese.

1 cup plus 1 tablespoon all-purpose flour

4 tablespoons unsalted butter, chilled and cubed

3 oz. strong blue cheese

½ teaspoon salt

½ teaspoon baking soda

1 teaspoon celery salt

2 teaspoons water

1–2 baking sheets, greased

Makes about 30–40

Preheat the oven to 300°F.

Put the flour, butter, cheese, salt, baking soda, and celery salt in a food processor and pulse until the mixture resembles crumbs. Add the water and pulse until the mixture comes together into a dough.

Transfer the dough to a lightly floured surface. Roll into a log about 1¼ inches in diameter, wrap in plastic wrap, and refrigerate for about 1 hour.

Remove the dough from the refrigerator and unwrap it. Cut into disks about ½ inch thick. Arrange the disks on the baking sheet(s), spacing them slightly apart as they may spread when they are baking.

Bake in the preheated oven for about 20 minutes, or until pale gold. Remove from the oven and let cool. Store in an airtight container for up to 2 weeks.

cheddar and apple straws

The tart apple in these straws gives them a lovely sweet and sour flavor.

1¾ cups all-purpose flour

5 tablespoons unsalted butter, chilled and cubed

3 oz. cheddar cheese, finely grated

1½ teaspoons salt

½ Granny Smith apple, peeled, cored, and grated

1–2 baking sheets, greased

Makes about 20

Preheat the oven to 325°F.

Put the flour, butter, cheese, and salt in a food processor and pulse until the mixture resembles crumbs. Stir in the apple and bring the dough together with your hands. Add water if it's dry.

Transfer the dough to a lightly floured surface. Roll into a log about 1½ inches in diameter, wrap in plastic wrap, and refrigerate for about 10 minutes.

Remove the dough from the refrigerator and unwrap it. Roll it out with a rolling pin on the work surface until about ¼ inch thick, then use a sharp knife to cut the pastry into ½-inch wide straws. Twist each one before spacing them apart on the baking sheet(s).

Bake in the preheated oven for about 20 minutes, or until pale gold. Remove from the oven and let cool. Store in an airtight container for up to 2 weeks.

spinach and chili straws

These crispy, fiery straws are to die for with a glass of cold beer and a light dip.

½ teaspoon ground coriander

½ teaspoon fennel seeds

½ teaspoon ground cumin

8 oz. fresh spinach (or 12 oz. frozen spinach, defrosted and drained)

1¾ cups all-purpose flour

6 tablespoons unsalted butter, chilled and cubed

1 small clove of garlic, crushed

½ teaspoon baking soda

½ teaspoon ground turmeric

¼ teaspoon ground cayenne or chili powder

1 teaspoon salt

1–2 baking sheets, greased

Makes about 20

Preheat the oven to 350°F.

Put the coriander, fennel seeds, and cumin in a dry saucepan over medium heat and leave for a minute or two until the seeds start popping, then set aside.

Blanch the spinach in a saucepan of boiling water for 30 seconds. Drain and squeeze to get rid of excess water. Chop finely. Put all the ingredients except the spinach in a food processor and pulse until the mixture resembles crumbs. Stir in the spinach and bring the dough together with your hands. Add water if it's dry.

Transfer the dough to a lightly floured work surface and roll it out with a rolling pin until about ¼ inch thick, then use a sharp knife to cut the pastry into ½-inch wide straws. Twist each one before spacing slightly apart on the baking sheet(s). Bake in the preheated oven for about 20 minutes, or until browned. Let cool. Store in an airtight container for up to 1 week.

parmesan and seed crackers

We've been selling these crackers since day one at our market stall on Portobello Road. Not only do they taste great, but they look fabulous too. I always have some at home and they're best enjoyed with a glass of white wine or Champagne.

1¾ cups all-purpose flour

¾ cup finely grated Parmesan cheese

1 teaspoon salt

1 teaspoon vegetable bouillon powder (or an extra ½ teaspoon salt)

a very small pinch of ground cayenne

5 tablespoons unsalted butter, chilled and cubed

3 tablespoons water

To coat the crackers

3 tablespoons sesame seeds

3 tablespoons poppyseeds

1 egg, beaten

1–2 baking sheets, greased

Makes about 40

Put the flour, cheese, salt, bouillon powder, cayenne, and butter in a food processor and pulse until the mixture resembles crumbs. Add the water and pulse until the mixture comes together into a dough.

Transfer the dough to a lightly floured surface. Roll into a log about 1½ inches in diameter, wrap in plastic wrap, and refrigerate for 10 minutes.

Remove the dough from the refrigerator and unwrap it. To coat the crackers, sprinkle the sesame seeds and poppyseeds over a clean tray. Brush the log with the egg and roll in the mixed seeds until evenly coated. Wrap the log in plastic wrap again and refrigerate for another 30 minutes.

Preheat the oven to 300°F.

Remove the dough from the refrigerator and unwrap it. Cut into disks about ¼ inch thick. Arrange the disks on the prepared baking sheet(s), spacing them slightly apart as they may spread when they are baking.

Bake in the preheated oven for about 25 minutes, or until pale gold. Remove from the oven and let cool. Store in an airtight container for up to 2 weeks.

See photographs on pages 96 and 97.

cheddar and chive crackers

This is another award-winning recipe for Popina. We make these crackers with vintage Somerset cheddar for the best flavor. They are particularly good eaten with a glass of red wine.

1¾ cups all-purpose flour

3 oz. aged farmhouse cheddar, finely grated

1½ teaspoons salt

⅛ teaspoon ground black pepper

5 tablespoons unsalted butter, chilled and cubed

3 tablespoons water

To coat the crackers

1 egg, beaten

3 tablespoons dried chives

1–2 baking sheets, greased

Makes about 40

Put the flour, cheese, salt, pepper, and butter in a food processor and pulse until the mixture resembles crumbs. Add the water and pulse until the mixture comes together into a dough.

Transfer the dough to a lightly floured surface. Roll into a log about 1½ inches in diameter, wrap in plastic wrap, and refrigerate for 10 minutes.

Remove the dough from the refrigerator and unwrap it. To coat the crackers, sprinkle the chives over a clean tray. Brush the log with the egg and roll in the chives until evenly coated. Wrap the log in plastic wrap again and refrigerate for another 30 minutes.

Preheat the oven to 300°F.

Remove the dough from the refrigerator and unwrap it. Cut into disks about ¼ inch thick. Arrange the disks on the prepared baking sheet(s), spacing them slightly apart as they may spread when they are baking.

Bake in the preheated oven for about 25 minutes, or until pale gold. Remove from the oven and let cool. Store in an airtight container for up to 2 weeks.

simple spelt and oat crackers

These crackers have a deliciously mild, buttery flavor and can accompany any cheese. I recommend stronger cheese varieties like blues, accompanied by the Beet, Fennel, and Apple Chutney.

1¾ cups spelt flour

1 cup rolled oats

½ teaspoon salt

½ teaspoon baking soda

6½ tablespoons unsalted butter, chilled and cubed

⅓ cup water

To coat the crackers

1 egg, beaten

2 tablespoons rolled oats

1–2 baking sheets, greased

Makes about 40

Put the flour, oats, salt, baking soda, and butter in a food processor and pulse until the mixture resembles crumbs. Add the water and pulse until the mixture comes together into a dough.

Transfer the dough to a lightly floured surface. Roll into a log about 2 inches in diameter, wrap in plastic wrap, and refrigerate for 15 minutes.

Remove the dough from the refrigerator and unwrap it. To coat the crackers, sprinkle the oats over a clean tray. Brush the log with the egg and roll in the oats until evenly coated. Wrap the log in plastic wrap again and refrigerate for another 30 minutes.

Preheat the oven to 300°F.

Remove the dough from the refrigerator and unwrap

it. Cut into disks about ¼ inch thick. Arrange the disks on the baking sheet(s), spacing them slightly apart as they may spread when they are baking.

Bake in the preheated oven for about 20 minutes, or until pale gold. Remove from the oven and let cool. Store in an airtight container for up to 2 weeks.

beet, fennel, and apple chutney

Sweet, sour, and delicately spiced, this gorgeous chutney is perfect with heavier cheeses and some of our crackers.

5½ oz. cooked beet, cubed

5 oz. fennel, trimmed and cubed

5 oz. sour apple, peeled, cored, and cubed

1 small red onion, cubed

¾ cup cider vinegar

1 cup sugar

½ star anise

2 cloves

1 teaspoon salt

2 x 8-oz. jars, sterilized (see page 4)

Makes two 8-oz. jars

Put all the ingredients in a wide saucepan and bring to a boil, then cook over low/medium heat for 1 hour, stirring occasionally. If after 1 hour the chutney hasn't reached a jam-like consistency, leave it to cook for up to 20 more minutes.

Spoon the hot chutney into the sterilized jars and seal immediately. Leave for 2–3 days before serving. Store refrigerated for up to 2 weeks.

spinach, garlic, and nutmeg muffins

8 oz. fresh spinach (or 12 oz. frozen spinach, defrosted and drained)

2 eggs

2¼ cups all-purpose flour

2 teaspoons baking powder

⅓ cup olive oil

1¼ cups whole milk

1 garlic clove, crushed

1 teaspoon salt

½ teaspoon ground black pepper

½ teaspoon ground nutmeg

a muffin pan, lined with 10–12 muffin cases

Makes 10–12

Preheat the oven to 325°F.

Blanch the spinach in a saucepan of boiling water for 30 seconds. Drain and squeeze to get rid of excess water. Chop finely.

Put all the ingredients, including the spinach, in a mixing bowl and mix until combined. The batter should be quite runny.

Fill each muffin case full with batter. Bake in the preheated oven for about 25 minutes. Do not be tempted to open the oven door halfway through baking as it might cause the muffins to sink. When they are ready, they should be well risen and springy to the touch.

Muffins are always best eaten warm from the oven, but if you have some left over you can refresh them with a quick flash in the microwave. Store in airtight container for 2–3 days.

feta and tomato muffins

2 eggs

2¼ cups all-purpose flour

2 teaspoons baking powder

⅓ cup olive oil

¾ cup whole milk

⅓ teaspoon vegetable bouillon powder (or an extra ½ teaspoon salt)

1 teaspoon salt

⅓ teaspoon ground black pepper

1 small handful of fresh parsley, chopped

3½ oz. feta cheese, crumbled

24 cherry tomatoes, halved

a muffin pan, lined with 10–12 muffin cases

Makes 10–12

Preheat the oven to 325°F.

Put the eggs, flour, baking powder, olive oil, milk, bouillon powder, salt, pepper, and parsley in a mixing bowl and mix until combined. The batter should be quite runny. Fold in the feta.

Half-fill each muffin case with batter. Pop 2 cherry tomato halves on top, then top up with batter to fill the case. Finish with another 2 tomato halves.

Bake in the preheated oven for about 25 minutes. Do not be tempted to open the oven door halfway through baking as it might cause the muffins to sink. When they are ready, they should be well risen and springy to the touch.

Muffins are always best eaten warm from the oven, but if you have some left over you can refresh them with a quick flash in the microwave. Store in airtight container for 2–3 days.

popina
**savory
tarts**

tart crusts

I rely on these three recipes for all of Popina's savory tarts. Pizza dough works very well during the summer, while a standard pie dough works better in the wintertime. For a richer flavor and healthier choice, I use spelt flour to make the pizza dough, even the pie dough.

pie dough

1½ cups all-purpose flour

6½ tablespoons unsalted butter, chilled and cubed

1 egg

⅛ teaspoon salt

1 tablespoon water

Makes enough to line a 9-inch tart pan

Put the flour, butter, egg, salt, and water in a mixer and blitz until it forms a ball of dough. If you prefer, you can make the dough by hand, but it's easier to do this if the butter is grated or very finely chopped.

Transfer the dough to a lightly floured surface and roll with a rolling pin until ⅛ inch thick. Line the pan with the pie dough and trim the excess neatly around the edges. Refrigerate for 20 minutes before using.

Turn to the tart recipe you are using and continue following the instructions.

pizza dough

1⅔ cups bread flour

1 teaspoon quick-acting dry yeast

⅛ teaspoon salt

2 tablespoons olive oil

1 egg

⅓ cup warm water

Makes enough to line a 9-inch tart pan

Mix the flour, yeast, and salt in a bowl. Make a well in the center and pour in the oil, egg, and water. Draw everything together with your hands until you get a soft dough.

Transfer the dough to a lightly floured surface and knead for a couple of minutes. The dough should be soft but not sticky. If it is sticky, add a little flour and knead again. Roll out the dough with a rolling pin until ⅛ inch thick.

Turn to the tart recipe you are using and continue following the instructions.

spelt pizza dough

1⅔ cups spelt flour

1 teaspoon quick-acting dry yeast

½ teaspoon salt

2 tablespoons olive oil

1 egg

¼ cup warm water

Makes enough to line a 9-inch tart pan

Mix the flour, yeast, and salt in a bowl. Make a well in the center and pour in the oil, egg, and water. Draw everything together with your hands until you get a soft dough.

Transfer the dough to a lightly floured surface and knead for a couple of minutes. The dough should be soft but not sticky. If it is sticky, add a little flour and knead again. Roll out the dough with a rolling pin until ⅛ inch thick.

Turn to the tart recipe you are using and continue following the instructions.

butternut squash and parmesan tart

This award-winning tart has been an essential part of our fall/winter menu for many years. Serve it as an appetizer or a delightful accompaniment to roasted meats and red wine.

1 Spelt Pizza Dough recipe (see page 106)

1 small red onion, thinly sliced

14 oz. butternut squash, peeled, seeded, and cut into matchsticks

⅔ cup heavy cream

1 large egg

3 tablespoons finely grated Parmesan cheese

1 teaspoon salt

⅛ teaspoon ground black pepper

a 9-inch loose-bottomed fluted tart pan, greased

Makes about 8 slices

Preheat the oven to 325°F.

Line the tart pan with the Spelt Pizza Dough but do not trim the edges yet. Set aside.

Put the onion and butternut squash in a mixing bowl, mix, and set aside.

In a separate bowl, put the cream, egg, cheese, salt, and pepper and whisk well.

Pour half the cream mixture into the tart crust, then scatter the onion and butternut squash over it. Pour in the remainder of the cream mixture. Now trim the excess pizza dough neatly around the edges.

Bake in the preheated oven for 30–35 minutes, until golden. Remove from the oven and let cool for a few minutes. Serve warm or cold.

goat cheese, tomato, and basil tart

With its light pizza dough base and fresh-tasting tomato, basil, and goat cheese filling, this is the perfect simple summer tart.

1 Pizza Dough recipe
(see page 106)

2 eggs

6 tablespoons Greek yogurt

3½ oz. sharp, soft goat
cheese, mashed

1 teaspoon baking powder

⅓ cup all-purpose flour

1 teaspoon salt

½ teaspoon ground black
pepper

2 tablespoons finely
chopped fresh basil

Topping

2 cups cherry tomatoes,
halved

1½ oz. sharp, soft goat
cheese, crumbled

olive oil, to drizzle

a few fresh basil leaves,
to decorate

*a 9-inch loose-bottomed
fluted tart pan, greased*

Makes about 8 slices

Preheat the oven to 325°F.

Line the tart pan with the Pizza Dough but do not trim the edges yet. Set aside.

Put all the ingredients in a mixing bowl and stir well until evenly combined and a soft consistency.

Spoon the filling in the tart crust and spread evenly. For the topping, arrange the cherry tomato halves all over the filling, cut side up. Finish by scattering the goat cheese over the top, then drizzle with olive oil. Now trim the excess pizza dough neatly around the edges.

Bake in the preheated oven for 30 minutes, or until tinged with gold. Remove from the oven, sprinkle with basil, and let cool before serving.

eggplant, bell pepper, and tomato tart

This deliciously easy tart is packed full of juicy summer vegetables. It's a good choice for a sophisticated picnic with a group of friends.

1 Pizza Dough recipe
(see page 106)

160 g baby eggplants,
halved lengthwise (or normal
eggplant, chopped)

2 large red bell peppers,
seeded and cut into strips

1 large red onion,
thinly sliced

3 tablespoons olive oil,
plus extra to drizzle

1 teaspoon salt

½ teaspoon ground black
pepper

⅔ cup cherry tomatoes,
halved

1 tablespoon freshly
chopped parsley

1 cup grated sharp cheddar
cheese

⅔ cup Greek yogurt

a 9-inch loose-bottomed
fluted tart pan, greased

Makes about 8 slices

Preheat the oven to 350°F.

Put the eggplants, bell peppers, and onion in a roasting pan (preferably nonstick), drizzle with oil, and season with the salt and pepper. Cover the pan with aluminum foil. Bake in the preheated oven for about 20 minutes, or until just soft. Remove from the oven and let cool, then chop the eggplant flesh (if you haven't already done so). Drain any excess juice from the roasted vegetables.

Reduce the oven temperature to 325°F.

Line the tart pan with the Pizza Dough but do not trim the edges yet. Set aside.

Stir the tomatoes, parsley, and half the cheese into the roasted vegetables and set aside.

In a separate bowl, mix together the yogurt and remaining cheese, then spoon into the tart crust.

Scatter the roasted vegetable mixture over the yogurt, spreading it evenly. Now trim the excess pizza dough neatly around the edges.

Bake in the preheated oven for 25–30 minutes. Remove from the oven and let cool.

bell pepper, pecorino, and thyme tarts

These light and summery tarts are packed with vibrant red and yellow bell peppers, as well as gutsy pecorino cheese and thyme. Enjoy with a glass of chilled, fruity white wine.

1 Pizza Dough recipe
(see page 106)

2 red bell peppers, seeded and cut into strips

2 yellow bell peppers, seeded and cut into strips

1 red onion, thinly sliced

2 tablespoons olive oil

½ teaspoon salt

½ teaspoon ground black pepper

2 garlic cloves, crushed

½ teaspoon freshly chopped thyme

½ teaspoon freshly chopped parsley

1 cup grated sharp cheddar cheese

2½ oz. pecorino cheese (1½ oz. grated and 1 oz. shaved)

⅔ cup Greek yogurt

5 x 4-inch nonstick tart pans

Makes 5

Preheat the oven to 375°F.

In a roasting pan, mix together the bell peppers and onion. Drizzle with oil, season with the salt and pepper, and cover the pan with aluminum foil. Roast in the preheated oven for about 20 minutes. Remove from the oven and drain any excess juice from the vegetables. Let cool while you line the tart pans.

Reduce the oven temperature to 325°F.

Line the tart pans with the Pizza Dough but do not trim the edges yet. Set aside.

Stir the garlic, thyme, parsley, ⅔ cup of the cheddar, and the grated pecorino into the roasted bell peppers and onion and set aside.

Mix together the yogurt and the remaining cheddar in a mixing bowl, then spoon into the tart crusts.

Scatter the roasted bell pepper mixture over the yogurt, spreading it evenly, and finish with the shaved pecorino. Now trim the excess pizza dough neatly around the edges.

Bake in the hot oven for 25 minutes. Remove from the oven and let cool.

honey-roast parsnip, carrot, and shallot tart

Plenty of roasted winter root vegetables with a hint of honey set in a light whole-grain spelt and olive oil crust. This makes a great rustic appetizer or accompaniment to winter roasts and stews.

1 Spelt Pizza Dough recipe (see page 106)

3 carrots, sliced on the diagonal

3 parsnips, cut into matchsticks

6 shallots, halved or quartered, depending on their size

1 tablespoon honey

3 tablespoons olive oil

1 teaspoon salt

½ teaspoon ground black pepper

1 cup grated sharp cheddar cheese

⅔ cup Greek yogurt

a 9-inch loose-bottomed tart pan, greased

Makes about 8 slices

Preheat the oven to 400°F.

Put the carrots, parsnips, and shallots in a roasting pan. Add the honey, oil, salt, and pepper and toss until evenly coated. Cover the pan with aluminum foil and roast in the preheated oven for 30 minutes. Remove from the oven, leave covered, and let cool for 10–15 minutes.

Reduce the oven temperature to 325°F.

Mix ⅔ cup of the cheese into the roasted vegetables.

Line the tart pan with the Pizza Dough but do not trim the edges yet.

Mix together the yogurt and remaining cheese in a bowl, then spoon into the tart crust.

Scatter the roasted vegetables over the yogurt, spreading them evenly. Now trim the excess pizza dough neatly around the edges.

Bake in the hot oven for 25–30 minutes. Remove from the oven and let cool.

port-poached pear, celeriac, blue cheese, and walnut tartlets

These nibbles pack a real punch—strong blue cheese with hints of port, walnut, and warm spices. They are ideal party canapés but I also recommend them with fine pork sausages at the holiday dinner table.

1 Pie Dough recipe (see page 106, but use spelt flour instead of all-purpose flour)

1 red onion, sliced

2 tablespoons olive oil

1 tablespoon water

1 celeriac (5–6 oz.), grated

½ teaspoon salt

½ teaspoon ground black pepper

¾ cup heavy cream

1 egg, beaten

3½ oz. strong blue cheese

¼ cup grated aged farmhouse cheddar cheese

1 teaspoon freshly chopped parsley

2–3 tablespoons chopped walnuts

Port-poached pears

2 firm Bartlett pears

1 cup port

3 tablespoons sugar

1 teaspoon whole cloves

2 star anise

1 cinnamon stick

3 cardamom pods, bruised

12 x 2-inch fluted tartlet pans (1 inch deep), greased

Makes 12

Prepare the port-poached pears 24 hours in advance. Peel and core the pears, then cut them into eighths. Put them in a saucepan with the port, sugar, cloves, star anise, cinnamon, and cardamom pods. Stir well and set over very low heat. Gradually bring to a boil, stirring occasionally, then cook for about 30–40 minutes. To check if they are cooked, prick them with a sharp knife—they should be soft but not falling apart. Remove from the heat and let cool in their cooking liquid, covered, for at least 24 hours.

When you are ready to make the tartlets, make sure you have lined the tartlet pans with the Pie Dough and refrigerate for 20 minutes while you make the filling.

Preheat the oven to 325°F.

Put the onion, oil, and water in a skillet and cook over low heat for about 6 minutes, or until soft and the water has evaporated. Add the celeriac, salt, and pepper and cook for 5 minutes, or until the celeriac has softened. Remove from the heat and let cool.

Put the cream, egg, and blue cheese in a bowl and mix with a fork, crushing the cheese as you go. Stir in the cheddar and parsley and mix well. Stir into the celeriac mixture.

Remove the tartlet crusts from the refrigerator and fill each one with the celeriac mixture. Scatter the walnuts on top. Take the poached pears out of their cooking liquid and arrange 2 pieces on top of each tartlet.

Bake in the preheated oven for 20 minutes. Remove from the oven and let cool.

mushroom tart

If you like to pick your own mushrooms, feel free to experiment with your selection, but you can just as easily use any seasonal variety you might find at your local farmers' market.

1 Pizza Dough recipe
(see page 106)

½ oz. dried porcini
mushrooms

1 large red onion, cubed

2 tablespoons olive oil,
plus extra to drizzle

2 tablespoons water

1 teaspoon salt

½ teaspoon ground black
pepper

1 teaspoon freshly chopped
thyme, plus extra whole
sprigs to decorate

2 garlic cloves, chopped

5 oz. white button
mushrooms (halved if big)

7 oz. cremini mushrooms,
sliced about ¼ inch thick

¾ cup light cream

1 large egg, beaten

*an 8 x 10-inch fluted tart
pan, greased*

Makes about 6 portions

Put the porcini mushrooms in a bowl of warm water and let soak for 20 minutes. Drain, chop, and set aside.

Preheat the oven to 400°F.

Put the onion, oil, and water in a skillet and cook over low heat for about 10 minutes, or until soft and the water has evaporated. Remove from the heat and stir in the salt, pepper, thyme, garlic, and porcini mushrooms. Mix well and set aside.

Put the fresh mushrooms in a roasting pan, drizzle with oil, and cover the pan with aluminum foil. Roast in the preheated oven for 10 minutes. Remove from the oven and let cool for 10 minutes. Drain any excess juice from the mushrooms, then stir them into the onion mixture.

Reduce the oven temperature to 325°F.

Line the tart pan with the Pizza Dough but do not trim the edges yet.

Mix together the cream and egg in a bowl, then pour half into the tart crust. Spread the mixed vegetables over the tart, then pour in the remaining cream mixture. Now trim the excess pizza dough neatly around the edges.

Bake in the preheated oven for 25–30 minutes. Remove from the oven and let cool, then decorate with a few sprigs of thyme. Serve warm or cold.

roast potato and scallion tartlets

Full of roasted new potatoes, these simple little tarts are a great accompaniment to spring lamb roasts, fish, or even soups.

1 Spelt (or regular) Pizza Dough recipe (see page 106)

1 lb. baby new potatoes, halved

3 tablespoons olive oil

1 ½ teaspoons salt

½ teaspoon ground black pepper

1 bunch scallions, sliced

2 garlic cloves, crushed

⅔ cup grated sharp cheddar cheese

⅔ cup heavy cream

1 large egg

6 x 4-inch fluted tartlet pans, greased

Makes 6

Preheat the oven to 400°F.

Put the potatoes, oil, salt, and pepper in a roasting pan and toss until evenly coated. Cover the pan with aluminum foil and roast in the preheated oven for 20 minutes. Remove from the oven and let cool for about 10 minutes.

Reduce the oven temperature to 325°F.

Stir the scallions, garlic, and cheese into the roasted potatoes and mix well.

Line the tartlet pans with the Pizza Dough but do not trim the edges yet.

Mix together the cream and egg in a bowl, then divide half between the tartlet crusts. Spread the vegetables over the tartlets, then pour in the remaining cream mixture. Now trim the excess pizza dough neatly around the edges.

Bake in the hot oven for 25 minutes, or until the filling looks golden. Remove from the oven and let cool for 5 minutes, then serve warm.

spinach, feta, and tomato quiche

Creamy with a generous amount of spinach and sweet cherry tomatoes.

1 Pie Dough recipe (see page 106)

6½ oz. fresh spinach (or 10 oz. frozen spinach, defrosted and drained)

½ cup crumbled feta cheese

1 garlic clove, crushed

½ teaspoon salt

½ teaspoon ground black pepper

2 large eggs, beaten

¾ cup heavy cream

½ cup lowfat milk

½ cup cherry tomatoes, halved

a 9-inch loose-bottomed fluted tart pan, greased

Makes 6 slices

Preheat the oven to 325°F.

Make sure you have lined the tart pan with the Pie Dough and refrigerate for 20 minutes while you make the filling.

Blanch the spinach in a saucepan of boiling water for 30 seconds. Drain and squeeze to get rid of excess water. Chop finely, then put in a mixing bowl with the feta, garlic, salt, and pepper and mix well.

In a separate bowl, mix the eggs, cream, and milk, then pour half of it into the tart crust. Scatter the spinach mixture over the top and spread evenly, then pour over the remaining cream mixture. Arrange the tomato halves over the top, cut side up.

Bake in the preheated oven for 30 minutes. Remove from the oven and let cool before serving.

leek and sharp cheddar mini quiches

So simple and yet so delicious; I suggest using a sharp farmhouse cheddar and young leeks when they are in season.

1 Pie Dough recipe (see page 106)

2 large eggs, beaten

¾ cup heavy cream

¼ cup lowfat milk

¾ cup grated sharp cheddar cheese

1 small leek, thinly sliced

½ teaspoon salt

½ teaspoon ground black pepper

6 x 4-inch fluted tartlet pans, greased

Makes 6

Preheat the oven to 325°F.

Make sure you have lined the tartlet pans with the Pie Dough and refrigerate for 20 minutes while you make the filling.

Put the eggs, cream, and milk in a bowl and mix well, then stir in the cheese, leek, salt, and pepper.

Remove the tartlet crusts from the refrigerator and fill each one with the leek mixture.

Bake in the preheated oven for 30 minutes. Remove from the oven and let cool before serving.

zucchini and fennel tart

Fresh and summery, serve with an arugula salad, fish, and white wine.

1 Pizza Dough recipe (see page 106)

12 oz. small zucchini, sliced ⅛ inch thick

1 small/medium fennel, trimmed and sliced ⅛ inch thick

1 small red onion, sliced ⅛ inch thick

3 tablespoons olive oil

1 teaspoon salt

½ teaspoon ground black pepper

1 tablespoon freshly chopped parsley

¾ cup grated sharp cheddar cheese

⅔ cup Greek yogurt

a 4 x 13-inch tart pan, greased

Makes about 6 portions

Preheat the oven to 400°F.

Put the zucchini, fennel, onion, oil, salt, and pepper in a roasting pan and toss until evenly combined. Cover the pan with aluminum foil. Roast in the preheated oven for 30 minutes. Remove from the oven, leave covered, and let cool for 10–15 minutes.

Reduce the oven temperature to 325°F.

Drain any excess juice from the vegetables, then mix in the parsley and about half of the cheese. Line the tart pan with the Pizza Dough but do not trim the edges yet.

Mix the Greek yogurt and remaining cheese in a bowl, then pour into the tart crust. Scatter the roasted vegetables over the top, spreading them evenly. Now trim the excess pizza dough neatly around the edges. Bake in the hot oven for 25–30 minutes. Remove from the oven and let cool.

See photographs on pages 128 and 129.

cheese burek

This wonderful Serbian specialty is taken from my mother Rozalia's collection of recipes and I have reworked it in two versions. It is easy to make and always impresses dinner guests. I recommend using strong, barrel-aged feta cheese for the filling if you can get it.

1 cup cottage cheese

2 oz. barrel-aged feta cheese, crumbled

¾ cup reduced-fat Greek yogurt

2 eggs, beaten

2 tablespoons olive oil, plus extra to brush

½ teaspoon baking soda

1 ½ teaspoons salt

6 large sheets of thick phyllo pastry (18 x 13 inches, see Note below)

an 8-inch springform pan (2½ inches deep), baselined with parchment paper

Makes 6 slices

Preheat the oven to 350°F.

Put the cottage cheese, feta, yogurt, eggs, oil, baking soda, and salt in a mixing bowl and mix well.

Make sure you have plenty of space to work on. Take one phyllo sheet and lay it on the work surface. Lightly brush it all over with oil. Place a second phyllo sheet on top. Spoon one-third of the cheese mixture on to the phyllo and spread it evenly across the surface, leaving the very edges clear.

Fold over each short side by 1 inch. Do the same with a long side, then carry on rolling it downward (not too tightly) until you've rolled all the phyllo and made a tube. Gently lift up the tube and curl around the inside edge of the springform pan. The phyllo tears easily so try to lift it gently, but don't worry too much if it tears a little.

Repeat this entire process with the remaining phyllo sheets, making 2 more tubes and fitting them end to end in the pan until you have a spiral. Brush the top with oil.

Bake in the preheated oven for 40 minutes until deep golden and risen. Don't worry if parts of the pastry look a little burnt —this tastes great! Remove from the oven and let cool for a few minutes. It freezes well—defrost and warm up in the oven before serving.

Note: The large sheets of phyllo pastry can be found in Middle Eastern stores or the freezer aisle of supermarkets. I let it defrost for 1 hour before I start. If you can't find such large sheets, simply overlap your sheets to make the correct size and remember that you'll need more to begin with.

spinach and cheese burek

I have been making this recipe for many years and it sells like hotcakes on my market stalls. Traditionally, in parts of Eastern Europe, burek is enjoyed with a glass of keffir, a type of drinking yogurt.

10 oz. fresh spinach
(or 1 lb. frozen spinach,
defrosted and drained)

½ cup cottage cheese

⅓ cup Greek yogurt

1 large egg, beaten

2 tablespoons olive oil,
plus extra to brush

2 tablespoons sparkling
water

½ teaspoon baking soda

1 teaspoon salt

6½ oz. large phyllo pastry
sheets

*a 7 x 7-inch baking pan,
greased*

Makes 4–6 portions

Preheat the oven to 350°F.

Blanch the spinach in a saucepan of boiling water for 30 seconds. Drain and squeeze to get rid of excess water. Chop finely, then put in a mixing bowl with the cottage cheese, yogurt, egg, oil, water, baking soda, and salt and mix well.

Lay a phyllo sheet in the base of the baking pan, leaving the excess pastry hanging over one side of the pan. Brush with oil. Lay another sheet on top so that the overhang is on the opposite side of the pan. Spread a generous tablespoon of spinach mixture over the phyllo sheet. Lay another 2 sheets over the filling and scrunch up the excess pastry to fit the pan. Brush with oil. Spread another generous tablespoon of spinach mixture over the phyllo sheet. Lay another 2 sheets over the filling and scrunch up the excess pastry to fit the pan. Brush with oil. Keep going until you've used up the spinach mixture. You should end with a layer of filling.

Finally, fold over the overhanging pastry to cover the top of the burek and brush all over with more oil. If the top isn't entirely covered with pastry, add another sheet and brush with oil.

Bake in the preheated oven for 40 minutes until deep golden and risen. Remove from the oven and let cool for a few minutes. It freezes well—defrost and warm up in the oven before serving.

smokey vegetable, lima bean, and paprika phyllo strudels

You can use different kind of beans for this recipe: as well as lima beans, pinto, flageolet, and navy are excellent too. I recommend serving this phyllo strudel with salads, soups, or a few slices of good cured chorizo.

3 tablespoons olive oil

1 small red onion, chopped

1 heaping cup cubed red and/or yellow bell peppers

½ cup cubed eggplant

½ cup cubed zucchini

8 oz. canned lima beans, drained and rinsed

½ teaspoon Spanish smoked paprika

1 teaspoon salt

⅛ teaspoon ground black pepper

1 garlic clove, crushed

2 small tomatoes, chopped

2 eggs, beaten

6 large sheets of thick phyllo pastry (18 x 13 inches, see Note below)

a baking sheet, greased

Makes 2—serves about 10

Preheat the oven to 350°F.

Heat 2 tablespoons of the oil in a skillet and cook the onion over medium heat for about 5 minutes. Add the bell peppers and cook for 5 minutes. Add the eggplant, zucchini, beans, paprika, salt, and pepper and cook for 10–15 minutes until the eggplant and zucchini have softened. Remove from the heat and let cool for 15 minutes. Stir in the garlic, tomatoes, and eggs.

Make sure you have plenty of space to work on. Take one phyllo sheet and lay it on the work surface. Lightly brush it all over with oil. Place a second phyllo sheet on top. Lightly brush it all over with oil. Repeat with a third sheet.

Divide the vegetable mixture in half and spoon one half along one longer side of the phyllo sheets, leaving a 1-inch gap on either side and spreading the filling about 2 inches wide. Fold the longer side of the pastry, nearest the filling, about 1 inch in, then roll the phyllo pastry up, tucking in the sides as you go. Brush the top of the strudel with a little more oil.

Repeat the entire process with the remaining phyllo sheets to make a second strudel. Place both on the baking sheet.

Bake in the preheated oven for 25 minutes. The strudels should be pale gold. Remove from the oven and let cool for 5 minutes.

Note: The large sheets of phyllo pastry can be found in Middle Eastern shops or the freezer aisle of supermarkets. I let it defrost for 1 hour before I start. If you can't find such large sheets, simply overlap your sheets to make the correct size and remember that you'll need more to begin with.

little margherita pizzas with olives

Imagine a bright summer's day, an alfresco lunch, chilled white wine, good company, and a leisurely afternoon ahead. The only thing missing is these little pizzas. Alternatively, it's Saturday afternoon on a crisp winter's day and you have no plans for the evening. Make up some of these, crack open a good bottle of red, and settle down on the couch in front of a movie.

First phase dough

¾ cup plus 1 tablespoon warm water

1½ teaspoons quick-acting dry yeast

1 cup bread flour

Second phase dough

1 tablespoon olive oil

1½ teaspoons salt

1¼ cups bread flour

Topping

1 cup strained tomatoes or tomato purée

2 tablespoons olive oil, plus extra to brush

1 tablespoon freshly chopped oregano, plus extra to decorate

½ teaspoon salt

¼ teaspoon ground black pepper

5 oz. mozzarella cheese, torn into pieces

¼ cup pitted black olives, chopped

2–3 nonstick baking sheets

Makes 16

To make the first phase dough, put the warm water and yeast in a mixing bowl and whisk, then add the flour and whisk again until well mixed. Cover and set aside in a warm place for 1 hour.

In the meantime, make the topping. Put the strained tomatoes, oil, oregano, salt, and pepper in a bowl, mix and set aside.

After 1 hour the first phase dough will be bubbly and have increased in size. For the second phase, add the oil, salt, and flour and mix well to form a dough. Transfer to a well floured surface and knead well for a few minutes. Divide the dough into 16 and roll each into a ball. Roll out with a rolling pin until you have a base about 4 inches in diameter. Put the crusts on the baking sheets and brush well with oil. Spread some of the tomato sauce over each crust and top with mozzarella and olives. Set aside in a warm place for about 30 minutes.

Preheat the oven to 400°F.

Bake in the preheated oven for about 12 minutes. Remove from the oven and scatter more oregano over the top. Let cool for a couple of minutes, then serve hot.

rustic focaccia with bell pepper and onion

Light and simple, this flavorful bread is great with soups and a tasty addition to your picnic basket.

1 envelope quick-acting dry yeast

1 cup warm water

3 cups bread flour

1 teaspoon dried basil

3 tablespoons olive oil

1½ teaspoons salt

Topping

3½ tablespoons olive oil

½ red bell pepper, seeded and thinly sliced

½ red onion, thinly sliced

an 8 x 12-inch baking pan or tart pan, greased

Makes 8–10 portions

Put the yeast in a glass measuring cup, then slowly whisk in the warm water and set aside for 5 minutes.

Put the flour, basil, oil, and salt in a mixing bowl and mix. Add the yeast mixture and mix well until you get a smooth dough. Transfer to a well floured surface and knead for a couple of minutes. The dough should be soft but not sticky. If it is sticky, add a little flour and knead again. Return the dough to the mixing bowl, cover, and let rise for 1 hour in a warm place. The dough should increase significantly in size.

Uncover your mixing bowl and transfer the ball of dough to the well floured surface. Knead well for a couple of minutes, then let rest for 5 minutes.

Roll out the dough with a rolling pin until big enough to fit your baking pan. Transfer to the baking pan and stretch it to fit snugly. Push your finger into the dough repeatedly to make dents about 1 inch apart all over the surface.

For the topping, drizzle the oil evenly over the focaccia and scatter the bell pepper and onion over the top. Cover and let rest for another 40 minutes. It will increase in size again.

Preheat the oven to 400°F.

Uncover the focaccia and bake in the preheated oven for 15 minutes—it should be pale gold. Remove from the oven and let cool. Store in an airtight container or bread bag for up to 2 days.

mini cornbreads with vegetables

These delicious and versatile little breads have a lovely light texture. They make great accompaniments to soups, salads, dips, or heavier roasted meats. They are so good you could have them any time: breakfast, lunch, or dinner.

1 egg, separated

1 cup nonfat milk

¾ cup vegetable oil

1 cup all-purpose flour

1¼ cups fine cornmeal

1 teaspoon baking powder

1 teaspoon salt

1 large red bell pepper, seeded and thinly sliced

9 cherry tomatoes, quartered

6 x 4-inch loose-bottomed fluted tartlet pans, greased

Makes 6

Put the egg yolk, milk, oil, flour, cornmeal, baking powder, and salt in a mixing bowl and whisk well until smooth. Refrigerate for 30 minutes to allow the cornmeal to soak up the liquid. This makes for better cornbread.

Preheat the oven to 400°F.

Remove the cornbread batter from the refrigerator. Put the egg white in a separate, grease-free bowl and whisk until it forms stiff peaks, then fold it gently into the batter. Spoon the batter into the tartlet pans almost to the top and scatter the bell pepper and tomatoes on top.

Bake in the preheated oven for 15 minutes. Remove from the oven and let cool before serving warm. Store in an airtight container for up to 3 days.

index

conversion chart

Volume equivalents:

American	Metric	Imperial
6 tbsp butter	85 g	3 oz.
7 tbsp butter	100 g	3½ oz.
1 stick butter	115 g	4 oz.
1 teaspoon	5 ml	
1 tablespoon	15 ml	
¼ cup	60 ml	2 fl.oz.
⅓ cup	75 ml	2½ fl.oz.
½ cup	125 ml	4 fl.oz.
⅔ cup	150 ml	5 fl.oz. (¼ pint)
¾ cup	175 ml	6 fl.oz.
1 cup	250 ml	8 fl.oz.

Oven temperatures:

120°C/130°C	(250°F)	Gas ½
140°C	(275°F)	Gas 1
150°C	(300°F)	Gas 2
160°C/170°C	(325°F)	Gas 3
180°C	(350°F)	Gas 4
190°C	(375°F)	Gas 5
200°C	(400°F)	Gas 6
220°C	(425°F)	Gas 7

Weight equivalents:

Imperial	Metric
1 oz.	30 g
2 oz.	55 g
3 oz.	85 g
3½ oz.	100 g
4 oz.	115 g
5 oz.	140 g
6 oz.	175 g
8 oz. (½ lb.)	225 g
9 oz.	250 g
10 oz.	280 g
11½ oz.	325 g
12 oz.	350 g
13 oz.	375 g
14 oz.	400 g
15 oz.	425 g
16 oz. (1 lb.)	450 g

Measurements:

Inches	Cm
¼ inch	0.5 cm
½ inch	1 cm
¾ inch	1.5 cm
1 inch	2.5 cm
2 inches	5 cm
3 inches	7 cm
4 inches	10 cm
5 inches	12 cm
6 inches	15 cm
7 inches	18 cm
8 inches	20 cm
9 inches	23 cm
10 inches	25 cm
11 inches	28 cm
12 inches	30 cm

acknowledgments

I'd like to thank the following people:

My friend and business partner Matt Gruninger for his dedication and support; all past and present Popina kitchen and market staff and drivers for their hard and dedicated work without whom Popina would not be here; Sergei Strelets and Laura Amos for their inspiration and hard work; in the office, Milena Velgosova and Karolina Wojtun; in the kitchen, Raphal Lukanski, Tibi Tehel, Magda Wozniak, Joanna Kawalerczyk, Tibor Varga, Bela Nagy, Graciano Vaz-Andrade, Kingsley Uyigue, Zsuzsanna Bimbo, Arthur Dzuiba, Tomasz Dyczko; Marion Gough for believing in us; Francesca Shepherd for all her help and work on PR; Igor Jocić for all Popina designs and his generous help over the years; Jose Lasheras for all Popina's own photographs; Johnny at The Print Factory for never letting us down; Patrick Cairns for his helping hand; all my friends who generously helped me in those first difficult years and throughout—Clare Pearson, Nick Henderson, Melissa Odabash, Jorge Camman, Tim Sanderson, Ryan Board, Susan Hicks, Hackney Business Venture for the initial grant and Mr Jonathan Miller at Fortnum & Mason who was the first buyer to notice Popina and who very kindly offered a helping hand. For their support and fine quotes, thank you to Elizabeth Hurley, William Sitwell, Editor of *Waitrose Food Illustrated*, Jenni Muir of *Time Out*, and Henrietta Green for her help and support over the years and for a lovely foreword. Thanks to Mark Handley and Cheryl Cohen from London Farmers Markets; Portobello Road Market Office; Louise Brewood from Broadway Market; to everybody at Ryland Peters & Small, in particular Alison Starling, Céline Hughes, and Steve Painter; book photographer Peter Cassidy; food stylist Linda Tubby; Jane Milton for testing recipes; to all our distributors and suppliers over the years and to all the fabulous Popina customers for their support and dedication; to my husband and my family. And last but not least, thank you to The Prince's Trust and His Royal Highness The Prince of Wales for the personal interest he has taken in Popina.